No Gangster More Bold

No Gangster More Bold

Murray Humphreys: the Welsh Political Genius Who Corrupted America

JOHN MORGAN

The Prince of Darkness is a gentleman.
Shakespeare, *King Lear*

Treat your crooked neighbour as you would
treat your crooked self.
Murray Humphreys

HODDER AND STOUGHTON
LONDON SYDNEY AUCKLAND TORONTO

British Library Cataloguing in Publication Data
Morgan, John
    No gangster more bold : Murray Humphreys, the
Welsh political genius who corrupted America.
    1. Humphreys, Murray   2. Crime and criminals
—United States—Biography
I. Title
364.1'092'4   HV6248.H78/

ISBN 0 340 26387 3

Hodder and Stoughton Editorial Office: 47 Bedford Square, London WC1B 3DP.

For Aled, with love
on his twenty-first birthday

Contents

DOWNTOWN CHICAGO An Impression

4

1

LITTLE SICILY

(Little Hell)

LAKE

MICHIGAN

DIVISION ST.

CHICAGO AV.

GOLD COAST

North Branch Chicago

CLARK ST.

Chicago River

LAKE ST.

RANDOLPH ST.

WASHINGTON 6 ST. 2

MADISON ST.

MONROE ST.

ADAMS 5 ST.

JACKSON ST.

VAN BUREN ST.

The Loop
(FORMERLY 'THE LEVÉE')

South Branch Chicago

3

CICERO

CLARK ST.

STATE ST.

WABASH AV.

MICHIGAN AV.

HOBOHEMIA

ROOSEVELT RD.

1. Humphreys' birthplace
2. Loop newspaper alleys
3. Al Capone's HQ (Cicero)
4. St. Valentine's Day Massacre
5. Federal Building
6. City Hall and public buildings

Illustrations

(between pages 92 and 93)

The author and publishers wish to thank the Chicago Historical Society (the St Valentine Day's Massacre) and the *Chicago Sun-Times* for permission to reproduce certain pictures.

Foreword

The quest for Llewelyn (Murray) Humphreys began in the desire to make a television documentary film about a vaguely-known gangster of Welsh origin who was thought to have been a colleague of Al Capone's. Only when we began making enquiries in Chicago did we discover that the man was more important than any histories of his epoch had proposed. Therefore, this biography has its origins in the researches made in the United States by my colleagues, Huw Davies, the Director of Programmes at HTV Wales, and by the documentary film's director, Don Llewelyn. In turn, they ascribe their enthusiasm to the work of the distinguished novelist Emyr Humphreys. As important as their contribution has been the help given me by Karen May of Chicago, particularly in building up the portrait of Humphreys from that city's newspapers during the years of his success. The film we made is entitled *It Takes a Crooked Man*; its Editor is Viv Grant. However, all three of my colleagues are absolved from responsibility, first for my choosing to present Humphreys as a man who achieved a potent form of the American Dream, secondly for those elements incorporated in the biography which depend on other reporting I have done from the United States, and lastly for my maturing view of that society.

However, I am indebted to them for introducing me to the important witnesses to the life of Humphreys. His daughter, Llewella, entertained us generously in Oklahoma; we did our best to respond in Wales. Her conversation is enchanting, her affection for her parents undimmed. Without her our film, as this book, could not have possessed whatever insights each may offer. The testimony of William Roemer, the FBI agent who pursued Humphreys long and who knew him well, invaluably supported an interpretation of the gangster's career which might have seemed high-flown: to wit, that the Welshman's talent was vital to the triumphs of the 'Outfit' or 'Syndicate' or 'Mob', as the Chicago hoods are variously entitled. The newspaper columnist Art Petaque was also an important, and entertaining, corroborator. The impressionistic map of Downtown Chicago was drawn for me by Garnet McClay.

I am grateful to HTV Wales for granting permission to quote from my recorded conversation with Llewella Humphreys – her maiden name – with Mr Roemer and Mr Petaque, and for the freedom to reproduce the Humphreys' pictures from the documentary film. Those authors whose works I found most useful in understanding a gangster who was so anxious to keep out of sight, are listed in the bibliography. I have a debt also to the Chicago newspapers and to the publications of the Chicago Crime Commission. In trying to portray a man who wilfully eschewed biography I needed all the help available, but realise that there remains so much more that he alone knew about American crime, law, business, trade unions, cinema and politics. Humphreys did not much distinguish between such various elements in his society. He was seldom wrong.

Mork
October, 1984

1 Humphreys: the great unknown gangster

Our interest's on the dangerous edge of things.
The honest thief, the tender murderer,
The superstitious atheist, demirep
That loves and saves her soul in new French books –
We watch while these in equilibrium keep
The giddy line midway: one step aside
They're classed and done with.

Robert Browning

Murray Humphreys, Public Enemy Number One, heir to
Scarface Al Capone's power, the brains of the so-called
Syndicate and the directing agent behind the muscle-men
and killers who have dominated numerous unions and
so-called trade associations.

Court Indictment, Chicago, June 1933

The politician as gangster is a familiar figure in history; the
gangster as politician is more unusual. Llewelyn Morris
'Murray' Humphreys is as brilliant an example of the second
category as any society could wish not to find. He introduced
crime into the bloodstream of American society. In the
opinion of those who pursued him for forty years, whether
police, the FBI, prosecuting lawyers, judges or murderous
rivals, this handsome and elegant, articulate and artistic, son
of Welsh-speaking migrants to Chicago was an incomparable
foe. His intellect graced his bombing, grunting, and psycho-
pathic Mafioso colleagues and his reckless Irish, killing
enemies; so much so that he made the gangster a part of

1

government. One FBI agent who pursued him for eight years at the particular behest of Attorney General Robert Kennedy, although knowing that Humphreys was a murderer, an acid-thrower, an intimidator and a corrupter of judges and politicians, and who met him fifty times, was beguiled by his charm and certainly moved at the news of the gangster's death. Humphreys died in 1965 at the age of sixty-six – of 'unnatural causes, a heart attack' as the Chicago wit Mike Royko put it in a savage obituary. The Welshman, in a long career, had survived all the bloody battles that had seen most of his friends and enemies shot down. He was a prodigy in the criminal battles of the poor in Chicago before Prohibition. He rose to riches through that moralistic spasm and bootleg liquor and, when it was done, he transformed crime in the United States from brutal hooliganism into a force that was to sway business and national affairs. 'No gangster was more bold' ran a banner headline when he died.

Immediately the question arises: if Humphreys was so powerful, if he exercised so important a role in twentieth-century American life, why is he so little known? The answer is contingent on several other answers which have much to do with the usual difficulty in offering any account of the Outfit. Most people in public life cherish secrecy: the gangster has better reason even than the politician or the company director or trade union leader to keep his affairs to himself. Maintaining accounts is not wise; keeping minutes of meetings is not to be recommended: even the threat of sudden death cannot always guarantee loyalty and trust. Thus, in piecing together an account of the behaviour of mobsters – even of the stature and renown of Capone's 'Outfit' or 'Syndicate' – there are contradictions about dates, times, the structure of organisation, meeting places, the ownership of brothels, saloons, and gambling establishments, whether to do with horse-racing, dogs, lotteries or, later, after Humphreys' triumph in Las Vegas, the slot machine and spinning wheel. Evidence at trials, eye-witness accounts, reminiscences of public officials: each for different reasons can be unreliable. Which politician would boast of his connection?

Historians dealing with the politician as gangster have less difficulty. In the European medieval period behaviour that in later epochs would be regarded as gangsterism was held to be the normal conduct of the State. The observation that political power comes out of the barrel of a gun might have been made by the twentieth-century Chinese leader Mao Tse-tung, but would have seemed a tedious cliché to combatants in Britain's Wars of the Roses, or indeed to any European king or baron in the years before the Enlightenment. Such periods are well-documented. Similarly in the present century the rise to power, and its employment, by Hitler, Stalin and Mussolini is set down in authenticated records. When the German communist poet Bertolt Brecht wrote his extended metaphor of the Nazi German triumph in terms of Al Capone and Chicago in *The Resistible Rise of Arturo Ui* he could be certain of his account of Hitler, less so of the true history of the Outfit. Brecht had not been to America when he wrote the play, such was the power of the Outfit's legend: more, Brecht had never heard of Humphreys.

To the biographer's general difficulty is added Humphreys' unique sensitivity. He was Browning's 'honest thief, tender murderer'. He eschewed fame. Had he chosen, when the authorities declared him the most important gangster after Capone, to have, like Capone, given press conferences and been available to foreigners for approbation, then he would have been treated as one of the most famous people in the United States. For that reason he retreated, not from power but from the limelight. His daughter suggested to me that he decided so because he thought it was stupid for the Outfit to be in the public eye. He was hard on colleagues who paraded their wealth. Many who were ostentatious were killed. Others went to jail for offences which could have been obscured but for vainglory. This would suggest that his concern was merely practical. Publicity was bad for business and therefore should be avoided.

Since it was one of Humphreys' serious achievements that he moved the Outfit's money into respectable American corporations once Prohibition was abolished in the early thirties, his distaste for publicity was fruitful. The principal engines of the most powerful economy in the world would not like it known that Humphreys was laundering money

3

from the criminal world to sustain them. (His enthusiasm for laundries and his role in fixing both owners and unions was vital in his career: he *invented* the concept of laundering money.) The cogency of his analysis might suggest though that it sprang from an intellectual gift alone. I suspect there was even more to it than that.

Let us suppose what it must have been like to be Humphreys. He was to be honoured among his peers in time as the 'brainy hood', 'the Einstein', 'Mr Moneybags' and flattered by the compliments of the Senate as being the most grave of gangsters, a far more serious enemy than the Mafia. He had known the Colosimos, O'Banions, Capones, Lombardos, Yales, all the world-famous hoods – and seen them shot or jailed. He had bought judges and lawyers and presidents' campaign managers. He had strolled around the White House, had thrown bombs at a president's father, had arranged the assassination of a Chicago mayor standing alongside President Roosevelt. He had bribed a state legislature to make gambling legal. He had so arranged things that the most powerful film studios in the world, in Hollywood, worked at his intimidation and had seen his colleagues in that enterprise go to jail while he himself was not even arrested. He had tutored the gangsters to plead the Fifth Amendment when interrogated by the Senate and been so pleased by his invention that he had hand-carpented the plea in his study at a house he built himself in Oklahoma.

There were other brilliant legal *coups*; there were horrible murders he committed or caused to be committed. Undoubtedly he was angry that in the sixties his old rival and colleague Joe Kennedy could not prevent his children, President John and Attorney General Robert, from harassing the Outfit: assassination was, as ever, the outcome. But even in the Outfit's dealings with the Kennedys he was urging less publicity, trying to restrain those – like his protégé Sam Giancanna – who sought the headlines by exchanging a mistress with President Kennedy. Humphreys arranged the transfer; Giancanna was murdered; Humphreys died of a heart attack.

Can it therefore only be a concern for the welfare of the Outfit that persuaded Humphreys to step back and manipulate the thugs and hooligans? I suggest that he may have comprehended Nietzsche's idea of the great man, of that power transcending the apparatus of power. People who knew Humphreys propose that he should have been a senator, so eloquent was he, so shrewd, so studious of world affairs. What a shame that he left school at the age of seven and mixed with the precocious hoodlums in the Loop in Chicago! His clever mother and idle but affable father would have brought with them from Wales the idea that politics is fun, a game for the bright – but also a means whereby the poor get even.

All this must be part of the answer to the question: why is Humphreys the unknown gangster? He would allow only his surname to be placed on his tomb in Oklahoma, so acute was his fastidiousness. He could carry a joke into eternity, yet his jokes (and many became celebrated) were never his undoing: nothing was his undoing. So, while it is the case that the standard histories of crime and politics in the United States in his great days from 1928 to 1965 carry scarcely a reference to Humphreys, research into the day-to-day murders, the critical court and Senate hearings, reveal that there was one figure ever present or, nearby, advising. More, conversations with the FBI or Chicago journalists or shy politicians sustain the view that here was the most serious American gangster of them all. He may have thought the grave a fine and private place: he was wrong.

A novel point of entry often offers an unexpected con-figuration. Those gangsters who have occupied the stage are there because they wanted fame. To approach Humphreys through his origins in Wales is suddenly to unmask him, is to recognise – from the evidence of the FBI, Chicago journalists and politicians and bondsmen and especially his daughter – that each regarded him as the most important gangster. More, those like Nitti, Accardo, Giancanna and the others in the Mafia who have been the subject of world attention were placed in their jobs by Humphreys. At the mob's board meetings, his was the decisive voice. If he became, as his daughter attests, weary of the game, he maintained among his acquaintance until the end a courtesy none of the animals he mixed with could pretend to. When FBI agent William

5

Roemer was charged by the Kennedys to find a way of arresting Humphreys, his first meeting with Humphreys took an odd form. Mr Roemer said he was upset that his children were being harassed by the Outfit. Humphreys expressed surprise and regret at this. He walked away across the Chicago River – this was 1958. A few days later he returned to the FBI agent and assured him that his children would not be harassed any more; some fool had made a mistake: he would not make the same mistake again. Other anecdotes about Humphreys' good manners are more bizarre. For example, when Humphreys and the famous murderer Sam 'Golf-Bag' Hunt were with some rich Chicagoan sportsmen after a day at the races in 1929, Humphreys, when Golf-Bag placed his false teeth in Humphreys' spaghetti, was regarded as being a real gentleman because he did not wing Golf-Bag with his surprisingly small revolver. (I have held it in my hand.) Legend has it that Humphreys said: 'Keep your teeth to yourself, Sam' – a very Welsh locution.

Once the suggestion was made that Humphreys had chosen the shadows, for however practical or mischievous a reason, then the evidence became available. Because historians had concentrated on the men who chose or were forced into the limelight, Humphreys became a footnote at most. The newspapers in Chicago, considered from a different point, offered sufficient evidence to sustain the thesis that Humphreys really is the key to understanding how a group who personified the Hobbesian appraisal of human and political life as 'nasty, brutish and short' could have helped to shape one of the two most powerful societies in the world.

Ascribing anyone's talent to genes is a dubious business. The temptation is strong for a Welshman to suggest that Humphreys in his manipulation of the most powerful gang of criminals the twentieth century has seen – apart from formal political forces like Hitler's or Stalin's – was playing a game familiar to his compatriots. It has been expressed in their favourite sport of rugby football, where the star is the outside-half or three-quarter. He is usually small and alert and can dance through the lunges of huge men. When Humphreys was born the heroes were the James Brothers – like him, curly marmosets; when he died the boys winning praise were Barry John and Gerald Davies. The tradition is strong. To dance as he did through the bullets and bombs, avoiding the carnage while helping, in his apprentice days, to organise it, might sustain a sentimental thesis. Like David Lloyd George, whose speeches his father heard when young, he clearly had that rare political talent to see first what was on the other side of the hill, even if he put the gift to perverse uses.

Before he died he risked his chances of returning to the United States by visiting his father's birthplace in Wales, a cottage grandly named *Y Castell* (the Castle). He took with him his first wife and his second wife. He filmed his travels, which is how I came to learn that he was a cinéaste who had made and edited, and created the sound-tracks for, substantial documentaries. A man so various that he seemed to be not one, but all mankind's epitome, perhaps. Nevertheless, what distinguished him from other political geniuses of his time is that he did shoot people with his own gun. In considering his career it is easy to be distracted – by his exploitation of a materialist society, and by his view that the respectable in America were corrupt – from the fact that for all that Humphreys is unknown, his achievement was majestic and sinister. He did not need to read Niccolò Machiavelli's classic handbook for the aspiring ruler – *The Prince*. It could not have taught him anything. But no warrior springs fully-armed from the womb. Where did Humphreys come from? From what kind of Welsh family background? What was the Chicago in which he grew into gangsterdom and wealth? Each formed him.

2 The Wales the Humphreys left behind

The future King Henry VII commanded his train to halt at a Welsh shepherd's cottage on the banks of the River Severn in the year 1485 because of the repute in which the humble man was held as a prophet. He asked him as to his future. '*Arglwydd* (Lord),' the Welshman replied, 'you will fight great battles and you will win.' When the King had departed the shepherd's wife said: 'Why be so foolish as to prophesy for the King?' 'Wife,' said the Welshman, 'if I am right, the King will reward me. If I am wrong, he will be dead.'

Montgomery legend, also ascribed to the poet
Dafydd Llwyd ap Llywelyn of Matharfarn.

A happy band on the hill slope
Were we that day, in high hope,
All at stretch and in good heart,
Resolute to play our part
With doughty deeds in winning fame
In men's mouths for Owain's name.
And there before the fray began,
In keen debate our talk ran
What part of profit each should gain
In booty when the foe was slain;
And ere a foeman hove in sight
Each averred, come what might,
Never yielding, he'd be found
Standing gloriously his ground.

The Battle of Waun Gaseg
by Llywelyn ab y Moel (d. 1440).

The Welsh are proud to think of their country as the Land of the White Gloves, an ancient place ambitious for peace, capable always of resolving grave issues with courtesy, employing the word where other Celtic nations reach for the gun. Frequently they contrast their history over the past two centuries with their neighbours, the Irish. On the whole, they propose that the Irish must have had a worse time of it, rather than search down the difficult alleys of enquiry where matters of religion or morbid sexuality may be uncovered. Certainly the day I arrived in mid-Wales, in the old county of Montgomeryshire, where that shepherd or poet had given such shrewd advice to the Tudor king five hundred years earlier, the hills and valleys were so peaceful as to deceive.

The great, clever gangster's parents Brian and Ann were born within ten miles of one another. The Humphreys' small farmhouse, more a cottage, stands on a low hill at Carno. Behind is Plynlimmon, the mountain that is Wales' spine. Here rise the Rivers Severn and Wye, two of the loveliest of Britain's waterways. In their early miles each springs over stones in bare, high land. The sheep inhabiting the country-side are peculiar. An eighteenth-century traveller reported on their strangeness without providing detail. I can only think that tradition or genetic force makes them still possess an angry shout and a belligerence that had me leaping a hedge to escape them. A shepherd explained to me that this nasty spirit among animals – usually figures of fun for their mind-less docility – was due to the local custom of feeding them by hand. Thus the sheep saw a human being as someone who was going to give them food yet did not approach in a spirit of gratitude but in fury that the benefactor had not arrived earlier.

When I arrived in the yard of the gangster's father's home a black lamb ran from the ruined barn. Legend, as ever, has it that a small fort once stood on the ground of *Y Castell* – some Celtic or Roman stronghold commanding a view of the valley and the territory towards England. The fact of the name carried weight with the family. When expatriate in poverty in Chicago, the Humphreys would talk of the Castle and the time when they would once more occupy so grand a name. Being born on the crown of hills in a cottage with

9

such a title can, not unreasonably, create enduring romantic confusions.

Brian Humphreys married a girl named Ann Wigley who lived even nearer the foothills of Plynlimmon. The farm was larger, but the land less lush: there are outcrops of rock within two hundred yards of the barn. Half a mile away are lead-mines, ruined now, but prosperous a century ago when the farmers' children married. The lead went to making bullets, roofs, and porcelain. Brian Humphreys and Ann Wigley were married in a Calvinistic Methodist Chapel in China Street – China being porcelain – in the neighbouring town of Llanidloes. Like most members of the Chapel they sang Handel's *Messiah* or the more recently popular *Elijah* by Mendelssohn and took part in the musical competitions at local *Eisteddfodau* which had become a feature of life among Welsh-speaking people in the late nineteenth century.

Most people in the place at that time spoke Welsh, the oldest living European language. In grammar and vocabulary it resembles Breton rather than the Gaelic of Scotland or the Erse of Ireland but sounds much the same to a foreign ear. The Humphreys, like a majority of their two million compatriots, also spoke English so that when they went to Chicago they did not share the language problems of the Poles, Germans, Italians and Swedes they found themselves among. Brian Humphreys spent some of his time as a cattle drover, guiding the animals from Carno to Llanidloes and beyond, to England. The principal market was at Shrewsbury. It was there that the verb 'to welsh' is held to have its origins. The English argue that it was the cunning, cheating behaviour of the Welsh drovers which led to the word's connotation. In turn, the Welsh allege that the verb means 'to cheat the Welsh'.

The culture which the Humphreys took with them to the United States was bewildering. An element was the powerful language of the Bible: each at home had a large copy of the good book in the Welsh language. In Welsh its eloquence has an even more apocalyptic force. Being Calvinistic Methodists they would, inevitably, have a sense of their own importance, perhaps moderated by a gloomy awareness of original sin and the knowledge that the quality of their sect's hymns

did not match more ebullient Welsh versions of noncon-
formity. This gravity in the contemplation of the next world
was curiously amalgamated with the familiar folk tales prevailing in the countryside. The Welsh Robin Hood, Twm
Shon Catti, had lived some three hundred years earlier on the
other side of Plynlimmon. If every Welsh child was brought
up to remember always to speak the truth, at the same time
he was to admire the cheerful bandit of the Towy caves. A
mild enterprise of Twm's is 'of how he stole a bull and sold it
back to its owner. Having stolen the bull he took it to market
to sell it, disguising the animal by fastening a long, bushy
artificial tail to its real tail. So clever was Twm that he
persuaded the real owner of the bull to buy it from him at
a goodly price.' There is another tale originating in the
Humphreys' part of the county which carries a more ambi-
guous, not to say baffling, message or, at best, one that does
no one much credit.

This tale, published under the title '*Twtti Glyn Hec*',
recounts how a poor widow named Mari and her baby
Robert are visited by a very old tall woman wearing a long
green cloak lined with red and a high black hat. She offers the
widow a fortune in gold if Mari would, in return, give her
the son. The witch, if such she be, says, though, that if Mari
discovers her name then she may have the gold and not lose
the baby. That evening Mari visits a wood and overhears the
witch dancing among a ring of fairies and singing. In the
course of the song she calls out her own name: Twtti Glyn
Hec. Mari runs home and soon the witch arrives. After
teasing the witch for a while, suggesting that her name is
Ceinwen or Nesta or Gwenno, she guesses correctly when,
according to the writer Eirwen Jones: 'There was a wild
scream. It seemed as though a great wind hurled around the
small kitchen, and in the draught the old witch flew up the
chimney.' Mari has her baby and the gold. The moral of
the tale would appear to be that in Montgomeryshire, whatever the Chapel might argue, you can have your cake and eat
it – or at least, if your intelligence service is good, you may.

The quiet of the countryside is misleading in other ways. It
was not in the youth of the gangster's parents as agricultural
as it is now. The lead-mines were busy attracting migrant

labour from England and Ireland. One of the world's richest coal-owners, David Davies of Llandinam, whose mines were becoming the most productive in the South Wales coalfield, began his career as a railway man in Llanidloes and Newtown nearby. This part of Wales had been one of the centres of the British woollen industry since the eighteenth century, its products shipped to the Americas. In the 1830s and 1840s the British government sent soldiers to Llanidloes to put down an insurrection. The radical Chartist movement was a serious force in Montgomeryshire. Here the established Church of England and the Tory landowners suffered serious political setbacks while Brian Humphreys and Ann Wigley were children. The Liberals, representing the Welsh smallholders and nonconformists suffering from English landlords, had produced their new champion in David Lloyd George. His message, however, offered on analysis some of the ambiguities and contradictions which mark the folk and religious culture. He was fond of calling his homeland a peaceful, civilised place – The Land of the White Gloves was a favourite of his – and yet in the same speech as he so beautifully spoke of peace he would remind his listeners of their history.

For my own part I cannot help believing that the prospects of Wales would be brighter and more promising were her destinies controlled by a people whose forefathers proved their devotion to her interests on a thousand battlefields with their hearts' blood, and a people who despite the persecution of centuries have even to this very hour preserved her institutions and her tongue, and retained the same invincible love for her hills . . . That is why I feel so sanguine that were self-government conceded to Wales she would be a model to the nationalities of the earth of a people who have driven oppression from their hillsides and initiated the glorious reign of freedom, justice and truth.

Of such was the language of politics in the youth of the Humphreys. Not that David Lloyd George was the first to offer such a prospect in the district. Newtown was the home of an earlier idealist, Robert Owen, a man who believed in decent wages for his workers and argued for trade unions when they were illegal. He believed that improved conditions in the factories and education would benefit employers and nation. 'If he had been listened to then,' the historian G. M. Trevelyan suggests, 'we should live in a different world today.' Within a few years, once they had arrived in Chicago, the Humphreys were to discover a dramatic perversion of Owen's ideas. At home the consequences of Robert Owen's thinking and practice were to make for a hectic political life.

Whether the triumph of Owenite thinking would have guaranteed prosperity to the small towns and hamlets of mid-Wales is less certain. The lead-mines went into decline in the 1880s; the demand for wool fell: agriculture went into a slump. What future was there for young people on the lower slopes of Plynlimmon? Where should they look for a bright prospect? Throughout the Welsh countryside the question was being asked – and answered usually by a migration within Wales, to the coalfields and the steel and tinplate works of South and South-west Wales. Here there was taking place one of the historic industrial expansions. The Humphreys decided to look westward and to emigrate across the Atlantic. They did not have the same pressure to go to the United States as say the Irish or Italians, since Wales, strangely, did not suffer a net migration of people towards the end of the century: indeed the population remained constant in numbers. But to the United States they went.

To think of going to the United States from what were landlocked small communities was not odd. The exporting of goods from small factories makes the exotic foreign place-names familiar. The port of Barmouth nearby had trafficked across the Atlantic for centuries. The Humphreys may not have been aware that more Welshmen signed the Declaration of Independence than any other people, or that great universities had been founded by compatriots, or that – as some historians had it – Prince Madoc had discovered the New World long before Christopher Columbus. But if all this scholarship was unfamiliar, they were capable of reading the advertisements in the local press telling when ships were leaving and how much a passage to a new life cost. The Welsh press offered several routes. The most popular ports of embarkation were Liverpool and Bristol. Living where they did, the Humphreys chose Liverpool even though it was crowded with even-more-impoverished Irish.

Strong Welsh communities existed in America, especially in Pennsylvania and Ohio. Welsh-language papers were published; chapels flourished, their ministers arguing against drink: there were Welsh saloons. Most of these migrants worked in the steel, tinplate and iron factories and in the coalmines, often as managers. The Humphreys chose to ignore these established centres and make directly for Chicago on Lake Michigan, the fresh crossroads and market of the new enormous nation. Brian Humphreys left behind in Carno his brother Llewelyn who was to become a dignitary of the county, a justice of the peace, a councillor. He was to name his second son after him, who would share his namesake uncle's interest in the law, but to what different, transforming ends!

3   The Chicago they found

Chicago is the second American city, the fifth German
city, the third Swedish, the second Polish . . .

G. W. Steevens, 1895

Chicago was corrupted the day the first Anglo-Saxon gave
the first bottle of whisky to a Red Indian.

Nelson Algren

Several European nations believe, with reason, that the
United States belongs to them. The English think they
have the strongest claim since a version of their language is in
common use. Germans are aware, although this awareness is
not universal, that it was only by the narrowest of votes that
their language did not become the official tongue of the new
power across the Atlantic; and what a difference it would
have made to modern history had that vote gone the other
way: would there have been a Hitler, a Second World War?
Italians and Irish and Jews of many nationalities feel a sense
of ownership. Presently, immigrants from the south of the
Americas will have a case. The Welsh – and it certainly must
have seemed so to the newly-married Humphreys when they
arrived in Chicago before the turn of the century – had
diminished in their influence after the early years of the
new republic. Unlike the other tens of thousands of new
immigrants to the Garden City, the Humphreys found no
community speaking their language to move into, to shelter
from the economic storm that was breaking.

Chicago's pioneering years were over, and an uproarious

adolescence had begun. In 1834 the Indians had been hood-winked out of their swamp land on the river. For trinkets and a few bottles of whisky Chief Sauganash abandoned a plot of land which was to be bought in 1844 for $8,000 and sold in 1852 for $3 million. For merchants and manufacturers of all kinds the path to the West and South was open to fortunes. Wheat and cattle moved through the city; coal and iron served it; the gamblers moved up the Mississippi and the Illinois and Michigan canal to accommodate such human frailty as the whorehouses left spare. In 1865 the *Chicago Tribune* suggested that 'the practice of shooting people upon the most trifling provocation is becoming all too prevalent in this city'. By 1890, as more and more refugees arrived from an impoverished Europe, the English-language newspapers were suffering from German, Polish and Swedish competitors. More than any other American city Chicago had produced the European crisis which brought people to it. It was the city of the new harvester and binder made by McCormick, one of her industrial moguls. As Professor Gwyn A. Williams writes in *The Welsh in their History*:

> The Americans invented the harvester in 1872 and the binder in 1880; they completed their vital transport net-work (with substantial help from British money). In 1887 on the wheat farms of the US north west with wages at $25 a month, wheat could be produced for 40 cents a bushel; in the Rhineland, with wages at 6 dollars a month, wheat cost 80 cents a bushel. The Americans could produce Indian corn in the Mississippi Valley, transport it to Italy and sell it there lower than that of Lombard and Venetian corn, where labourers were paid a third of US wages. In 1885, 77,000 Italian farm labourers emigrated to the USA. During the 1880s over one and a quarter million people left rural Germany and over half a million quit Scandinavia; Denmark had to rebuild itself.

What an irony, then, for the migrants, driven from home by the consequences of the McCormick reaper and binder, to arrive to discover workers shot down at the gates of the very factory which had, so distantly, contributed to their poverty.

Even when the Humphreys arrived, six years after the Haymarket Bomb, Chicago was dominated by that explosion's consequences. The McCormick workers had been killed because they were striking for an eight-hour day and higher wages – or, rather, out of a fear that wages would be lowered because of the great numbers of new immigrants coming on to the labour market. The language of their protests was mostly German. The *Arbeiter Zeitung* was the main socialist paper: the English-language newspapers called it anarchist. The press now, as later, was far more ferocious in its attacks on workers than were the supposedly corrupt Chicago political leaders – possibly because the former cared for advertising from capitalists, the latter for votes and cash from the people: or possibly because each had higher motives.

The *Arbeiter Zeitung* called a protest meeting in the Haymarket. The mayor was not troubled, nor was the governor of Illinois. One police lieutenant took a different view. There was a fight. Someone threw a bomb and created a tradition. The socialists or anarchists believed it came from the hand of an *agent provocateur*. The law hanged four. All – Parsons, Spies, Fischer and Engle – made strong speeches, but in the opinion of union leaders Parsons did not help the cause of those who remained by arguing for the virtues of dynamite. What kept the memory of the Haymarket affair warm was the fashion in which the English-language press used it when the next big strike came in 1894; and in the question of whether the new Governor Altgeld would pardon those convicted but not executed. The compassionate near-socialist governor did and so finished his political career.

Before the Pullman strike in 1894 which was to be so instructive to the Humphreys – as to all the other new migrants in Chicago – they were to gather that they really had come to a theatrically rich city. Without parades and festivals Chicago was awesome enough. The old frontier town had been destroyed in the Great Fire of 1870 (as with everything else, its fire had been the greatest known) and already its new skyscrapers were the most distinguished. The architect Louis Sullivan had built according to local theories of rule-by-the-people, held to distinguish the Chicagoan school in all the arts. Then, as now, the fine palaces built along State and

17

Madison and the other thoroughfares delight the eye; they strike dumb: they may have been then, as now, difficult to live with in their majesty. Height helped, given the cost of land. The engineering genius of Root, Burnham and Le Baron Jenney went hand in hand with that of Sullivan. The Cable Street Chapel in Llanidloes in which the Humphreys had married, the tallest building in that town, would have reached the second storey of a Sullivan building on Madison. A lot later the Humphreys were to learn with surprise that the only community to grow as quickly as the new home they had come to was that part of Wales not far south from the village they had left. Chicago's population, then one and a half million people, had been a couple of thousand in an Indian homestead sixty years before; South-east Wales grew as fast.

As well as rich, Chicago was, the Humphreys were to learn, as wild and disreputable a town as modern times had seen. They had moved into a flat on Clark Street, just a few doors away from a garage where in 1929 the St Valentine Day Massacre was to be staged, in which their as-yet-unborn son Llewelyn (named after his father's brother back in Wales) was held to be involved. Clark Street was one side of a rectangle – Wabash, Twenty-Second and Eighteenth were the others – which held the area known as the Levee.

So when the young Humphreys took a stroll towards the lake of an evening and came to the Levee they would find, according to Emmett Dedmon in his *Fabulous Chicago*:

> Gambling houses, barrelhouse saloons, dance halls, pawn shops, tintype galleries, voodoo doctors, penny arcades, fake auctions and a few legitimate livery stables, blacksmith shops and oyster bars. Within the borders of a few blocks were located more than two hundred brothels. They ranged from low dives and panel houses, where robbers worked in collaboration with prostitutes, to elegantly furnished mansions governed by a strict code of conduct. A visitor to the Levee usually said he was 'going down the line': he was lucky if he returned with his bait.

This clears up the puzzle of what Frank Sinatra means when, singing the twenties 'Chicago' in concert, he has an aside about 'going down the line'. Also perhaps about where Mr Brian Humphreys acquired the gambling habit, which was later to be subsidised daily by his prosperous younger son.

The Levee, so-called by the dashing professional gamblers who had come from the South after the Civil War, was not to make its unique mark nor to impose its style on Chicago politics for more than another decade. In 1893 enthusiasm was directed at demonstrating to the world that Chicago was the American city with the mostest. Hadn't the Iron Chancellor Bismarck said that he would like to go to America if only to see that *Chicago*? How much more would he wish so, once they had staged the exhibition to celebrate Columbus' discovery of America. So elaborate were the plans that it would have to happen a year later than it should have done: what did that matter?

And so it came to pass that almost seven hundred thousand citizens of Chicago followed their Mayor Harrison, the President of the United States and a descendant of Columbus, the Duke of Veragua, southward to the exhibition's White City, built (like Venice) on a beach. It was May Day and the crowds were to come from all over the United States until late October. The Infanta of Spain came; so did Archduke Ferdinand, heir to the Austro-Hungarian empire; the Queen of Italy sent laces which had not travelled out of Italy before, finery the Romans had stolen from Egyptian tombs in Caesar's time.

Most European nations had sent exhibits to the Exposition. Since Chicagoans were in permanent competition with Yankees on the East Coast for universal regard, these manifestations of sophisticated enthusiasm delighted more than the wealthy. Not, they'd have you know, that they paid much attention to what the Bostonian or New Yorker might think about anything. Indeed, the Chicago newspapers seldom reported events outside their domain. (They still don't over-tax any reader's concerns abroad.) But, on the other hand, the patronising tone of the Eastern previews of the famous event had been insufferable. For example: Chicago women did not know how to dress. At their parties they did not have people who knew even how to pour wine properly.

19

But my, my, hadn't the snobbish New Yorkers been shown up by events. So how sad that, on the very day the Columbine jamboree concluded, the city's popular Democrat Mayor Carter Harrison, the man who had fought off a Republican with a plan to close the Levee during the Exposition, their local hero should be murdered by an assassin with no serious complaint in his demented mind. If this canker in the rose of the year was to distress and impress the new immigrants, its malignant spread within months was to touch them more nearly.

The tough, dreadful working conditions in the stockyards and factories of Chicago at the turn of the century were to be described by novelists Theodore Dreiser and Upton Sinclair with such force, with such impassioned detail, as to create a new kind of literature. The Humphreys family from mid-Wales were to be the raw material of transforming fiction, always a less satisfying role. They worked in the stockyards; were caught up in the trough of that cycle of depression and boom which then, as now, is governed throughout the world by the mysterious spirit of the United States' market. For the Humphreys, though, the historic conflict they migrated upon in Chicago in the early nineties was peculiarly poignant.

George M. Pullman, the railway baron who provoked a murderous strike, was an uncannily perverse capitalist image of the Robert Owen of their homeland. Owen was the employer who believed in the goodness of man, in the common weal. Ten miles from Chicago George Pullman built a city in his own name for his workers, one as attractive in design as anything Owen might have wished: it was just that his purpose was different. It sounded good:

> Such advantages and surroundings make better workmen by removing them from the feeling of discontent and desire for change which so generally characterise the American workman, thus protecting the employer from the loss of money and time and money consequent upon intemperance, labour strikes and dissatisfaction which generally result from poverty and uncongenial home surroundings.

The difference between the Pullman dream and the Owenite was soon brought home to the Humphreys, as to those Chicagoans who were shot down in the course of the distinction's revealing. In the Depression of 1893 and 1894 demand fell on the railway. Pullman wanted to reduce wages. In the stockyards men were laid off. Pullman's workers at once argued that they were barely, anyway, making a living wage. Now Pullman was reducing wages in his new Utopia: he was not reducing his rents or his charges for electricity and the rest of life's necessities. His was a feudal not an Owenite Utopia. His impoverished workers went on strike.

'Within two weeks,' as *A History of the American Labour Movement* has it,

> a sequence of events began that was to bring against the new united Railway Union all the resources that monopoly could throw against it – the United States government, the President of the United States, the United States Army, the Attorney General, the courts, the prisons, bullets and the press which outdid itself in describing what it called the 'Debs Rebellion' [Eugene Debs was the union leader]. No matter how it is viewed it is an extraordinary chapter in American history. Because a trade union, with unusual generosity, tried to help some starving factory workers, all the forces of the established order were released to crush it and imprison its leaders.

Undoubtedly it was 'an extraordinary chapter in American history', but one that was to have a far more subtle set of consequences for Chicago, and eventually for the United States, than any straightforward Marxist reading of a struggle between brutish capitalism and syndicalist socialism might suggest. Within the general railway strike which spread throughout America were contained uniquely Chicagoan features. The attorney general serving President Cleveland in Washington was Richard B. Olney, who had been a member of the board of a Chicago railway involved in the strike. He had been the lawyer for six other railway companies. He decided to send US Army platoons into Chicago even though Governor Altgeld told him not to. In spite of the protests of the Chicago superintendent of police, Attorney General Olney encouraged the swearing in of deputy-marshals in the bars and brothels of the Levee: he had guns put in the hands of ex-convicts, thugs and thieves and encouraged them to shoot strikers: they did.

In July 1894 the Humphreys' new home city held 14,000 armed men: 6000 troops, 5000 railway deputy-marshals and 3000 police. The hooligans from the Levee provoked quarrels; strikers responded. Thirty men and women were killed and, by varying accounts, one or two hundred wounded or injured. Consequently Eugene Debs and other union leaders were arrested. Their principal crime was in organising the strike across state lines. This was held to be an offence against Anti-Trust laws. Naturally this legal opinion caused surprise among those citizens who had seen flourish the trusts freely created by John D. Rockefeller, J. P. Morgan, Andrew Carnegie and others whose agents had shot down a few strikers in their time.

The new migrant could make a judgment that perhaps in this new land there was one law for the rich and one for the poor. But he had thought that back in Wales. Here, though, it seemed to be the case that a man in Washington, wherever that was, working for the president, could send in troops and organise the kind of criminal who lived just down the street from him on Clark or Madison and give him an official gun, even though the local governor and sheriff objected. That was interesting. It wasn't like that exactly in Wales, even if life there hadn't been all it should be. But, coming from Wales, where for better or worse a political sense is the sixth a man or woman is born with, the Humphreys could observe that in their new home there were voices with the eloquence of their preachers and politicians in the Welsh language. There was the voice of Clarence Darrow. He was another railway lawyer in Chicago, one nauseated at the conduct of his former colleague, Attorney General Olney. Darrow came to the defence of the union leader Eugene Debs and began then to refine a language which was to make him immortal a few years later in his peroration to a jury defending another union leader, Big Bill Haywood, against a charge of murder:

I speak for the poor, for the weak, for the weary, for that long line of men who in darkness and despair, have borne the labors of the human race. Their eyes are upon you twelve men of Idaho tonight. If you kill Haywood your act will be applauded by many. In the railroad offices of our great cities men will applaud your names. If you decree his death, amongst the spiders of Wall Street will go up paeans of praise for these twelve good men and true. In every bank in the world, where men hate Haywood because he fights for the poor and against the accursed system upon which the favored live and grow rich and fat – from all these you will receive blessings and unstinted praise.

But if your verdict should be 'not guilty' in this case, there are still those who will reverently bow their heads and thank those twelve men for the life and reputation you have saved. Out on our broad prairies where men toil with their hands, out on the broad ocean where men are tossed and buffeted on the waves, through our mills and factories and, down deep under the earth, thousands of men and women and children – men who labour, men who suffer, women and children weary with care and toil – these men and these women will kneel tonight and ask their God to guide your hearts.

The vigour of the Chicagoan Darrow's advocacy won Bill Haywood's acquittal and many other victories for besieged trade unionists, so much so that it might be supposed his would be the prevailing tone among immigrants in their attitude towards the unions. There were several haunting episodes which suggested that it might be so. When Eugene Debs returned to Chicago from jail a crowd of 100,000 people came to meet him at the railway station: 'They wept, cheered, laughed and cried.' When George Pullman died, three years after he had broken the union in the 1894 strike, he was buried at night in a deep tomb, the coffin covered with concrete reinforced by steel. Out of a fortune of $18 million, he left his sons $3000 a year since neither had shown that seriousness 'requisite for the wise use of large properties and considerable sums of money'.

How then does the shrewd migrant, by nature indolent,

imbued with the mordancy of Calvinism's sense of original sin, making – just – ends meet in the stockyards, how then does he interpret these thunderous battles in a city about to become one of the wealthiest the world has known? That all flesh is grass the Chapel has taught him. But there *is* that time in between. He hears quoted that noble remark of his new country's saviour and his state's hero, Abraham Lincoln: 'Liberty before property; the man before the dollar.' Yet Chicago's question has it: 'If you're so smart, why ain't you rich?' He lives in a city that is to give many new words to the language but knows a few already in universal use. For example: Mickey Finn kept the Lone Star Saloon at the southern end of Whisky Row. His Special was a cocktail of beer, pills from a voodoo doctor and water with a touch of snuff. This would knock a man cold for two days, when he would be dumped in a room with other dopes, while Mickey emptied their pockets in his time spare from serving at the bar. If the Humphreys themselves were not to make sense of this rich culture, their son Llewelyn, born just before the century's end, had little difficulty. Indeed he was to resolve the conflict between capitalist and trade union in a uniquely disgraceful fashion, one which the original robber barons such as Rockefeller, Vanderbilt, Morgan and Pullman would have found astonishing, while eloquent idealists like Debs, Haywood, Jim Hill or Darrow would have been shocked: he was to exploit both.

4 The mobs before Prohibition

Chicago: first in violence, deepest in dirt, loud, lawless, unlovely, ill-smelling, irreverent, new, an overgrown gawk of a village, the 'tough' among cities, a spectacle for the nation.

Lincoln Steffens

Black Powder Bombs $100
Dynamite Bombs $500
Guaranteed Contracts $1000

Chicago mob tariff, 1920

The Democratic party (in Chicago) is built upon bribery, intimidation, bulldozing of every kind, knifing, shooting and the whole swimming in whiskey.

William T. Stead, 1893

Llewelyn Morris Humphreys was born in April 1899, the second son of parents who were never even to try to become American citizens. Until their son became notorious, this hedging of bets, this passion for their homeland, was of little interest to anyone since they were people of no account. Subsequently it was to be thought an odd trait, this lack of any desire to be members of the greatest nation on earth. They had from the beginning little control over their bright and belligerent son. Coming from a society where every parent's ambition was to see a child do well in the new order of schools, into a chaos where strong, if ineffective efforts were being made to create a new America through education, they threw up their hands. Llewelyn left school at the age of seven and never returned.

25

Later, when Presidents Truman and Eisenhower were to remark on what a cultivated and educated man he seemed, especially for a mobster chief, Llewelyn would claim that he had been to high school, even to college: it was not true.

Seven is an impressionable age; for many of us a taste for music or games is formed then and endures a lifetime: Freudians would propose that the betrayal of Christ was created in the childhood of Judas. (Non-Freudians should respond that Judas did not *have* to do it.) At seven Humphreys was selling newspapers in the Loop in Chicago. His motive might well have been to earn some money to help his impoverished parents since there is enough evidence that he was generous towards them throughout their life. The consequence of this innocent, childish wish was a startling, physical awareness of life in the asphalt jungle, as American cities came to be known; those twenty thousand streets under the everlasting Chicago sky.

To offer newspapers for sale in Chicago in 1907 was not a simple matter of the papers being dropped at a street corner and placing them on your stall, or running with them under your arm and offering them to a customer. If you were a *Tribune* boy you had to watch out for the *Herald-Examiner* boy and watch out for yourself. As your batch of papers arrived a few thugs might arrive simultaneously and try to snatch them from you. Therefore you needed a few heavies in your support. It might be that your copies would never arrive. Even between the presses on the Chicago River and your corner in the Loop the truck could have been hi-jacked and set alight, the middle-men thumped unconscious. Journalism was not exempt from the operation of the Chicago interpretation of market forces. The principal exponent of thuggery in newspaper selling when Humphreys was seven years old was the sixteen-year-old Dion O'Banion who would, when Prohibition came, be the leader of the Irish gang against the Italians and their new boss Al Capone.

In the years between starting to sell newspapers in Chicago and being sent to jail at the age of eighteen for theft, Llewelyn Humphreys was taken up by a Chicago judge, Jack Murray. His life was to be transformed. Usually in history, when accounts are written of a meeting that leads to a higher upland, to a revelation, or even to a sweet trip down a primrose path, we comprehend the character of the transformation. When Faust meets Mephistopheles we know what is in store; similarly what happens to Keats on first opening Chapman's *Homer*; Bunyan was clear about *Pilgrim's Progress*. Defining the Humphreys experience is more unusual. Here was the adolescent petty crook; there was Judge Murray, a junior figure in the electoral confusions of Chicago law, a bachelor, otherwise unremarkable. One consequence might have been that for Humphreys the judge offered the possibility of a law-abiding life. The thief might have seen the error of his ways. Or he might have amended his ways slightly and become a Chicago lawyer. What seems to have happened is rare, surely? Humphreys did learn lessons from the judge but they were lessons that were to legalise crime, pervert justice, hold up to American society a mirror so mocking as to upstage not merely Caliban but the Senate, even the presidency. To honour the judge, Humphreys abandoned his Christian names Llewelyn Morris – he was to be known ever afterwards as Murray. Quite where and when the newspaper seller met the judge is unknown: Humphreys did not go into detail. The best guess is that it was in 1913, when Humphreys was thirteen. Given the democratic system whereby judges, like district attorneys and other officers of the law, are elected, the judge would have taught young Llewelyn Morris Humphreys as much about the political system as law, the two being scarcely distinguishable.

The young criminal, like most young people, is not usually interested in the politics of local government. If there is a shop to be robbed, a bank raided, a citizen to be kidnapped, a family to be intimidated or, as he grows in his trade, a rival to be shot, then a study of the balance of parties in City Hall would not normally seem to be required knowledge. In Chicago, however, in Humphreys' youth civic studies were peculiarly important. Even without the insights offered by Judge Murray a brief reading of the newspaper headlines he offered for sale would have impressed the young Humphreys. In the mayoral election of 1915 there had been an upset: the Democrats had been defeated. More, a mayor had been elected so maverick in his loyalties and, even for the great city, so extravagant in his

changes of mood and policy as quite to confuse the underworld. This mayor was Big Bill Thompson.

Until his election certain decencies obtained. The place had
been run since the turn of the century by two Democrats – John
'the Bath' Coughlin and Michael 'Hinky Dink' Kenna. The
Bath owed his nickname to being the proprietor of the bath-
houses, meeting places of political importance since, like bars,
they encouraged conversation. Hinky Dink meant a little
fellow, well-met. Each had come to power through the Irish
connection and its consequent extension of the Irish belief that it
was the duty of a family to help itself. This Irish Catholic view
of politics – to be supported by the comparable Italian Catholic
attitude – was also important in Boston and New York as,
later, in Dublin. Protestant concepts of objective fairness or
justice, the disinterested judgment between contestants, which
had been aimed at by the founders of the United States, were
alien to the spirit of Chicago.

The Bath and Hinky Dink gave parties of a kind so vast that
by the second decade of the century the police had called a halt.
They controlled the First Ward which covered the Loop. Each
was an alderman. They had made graft or, as it was known to
them, boodle, the accepted grease in the wheels of government
and trade. Even in 1910 an alderman could expect to make
$20,000 a year helping along a contractor or an insurance agent.
The Bath and Hinky Dink had gathered around them a crowd
of aldermen, which one Chicago mayor described as a 'low-
browed, dull-witted, base-minded gang of plug uglies with no
outstanding characteristic beyond an unquenchable lust for
money'. The gangster Big Jim Colosimo was an ally.

As the mayoral election of 1915 approached, Big Jim, Hinky
Dink and the Bath, although powerful, were uneasy. The year
before there had been bad publicity for a murder arranged in
the Levee. Mayor Carter Harrison II, the first Chicago-born
citizen to hold the office, had proved a disappointment.
Although one of the boys, a true Democrat, he had been siding
with reformers. He had helped to bring about the banning of
brothels in Chicago; the Levee was to be closed. Not that the
law actually made for much change. Big Jim Colosimo had,
one day, contributed to the debate by sending hundreds of his
whores in all their most spectacular finery into the restaurants

of the city and suburbs, as if to suggest that such would be life after the Levee was closed. Losing that argument, he set up brothels in the suburbs. Business was not much affected by reform.

However the mayor, aiming high for probity, had also caused several friendly police officers to be sent to jail. This was a serious matter for Colosimo and indeed for the aldermen: it suggested politicians could not be relied upon. Mayor Harrison then set up a Morals Squad under Major Funkhouser and Inspector Dannenberg, a move that disturbed Captain Michael Ryan of the Twenty-Second Street Police Station whose graft or boodle derived from the Levee brothels. Big Jim sent out two gunmen, Chicken Harry Gullet and Duffy the Goat, to put an end to the threat. Captain Ryan brazenly circulated the picture of his new colleague Inspector Dannenberg among friendly hoods so that they would recognise the man they had to injure or kill. The result of these manoeuvres was an attack by the mob while Inspector Dannenberg was arresting prosti-tutes and panders. Two policemen were killed. The Chicago *Tribune* blamed Hinky Dink, the Bath and Captain Ryan. Big Jim Colosimo was arrested but never charged. Mayor Harrison, though, did move the corrupt Captain Ryan, and even appointed an honest officer; many brothels were closed. But the *Tribune*, Republican as ever, was not assuaged. It had joined the name of the reforming Mayor Harrison with Hinky Dink and the Bath, and by inference, Colosimo. They were all guilty men. The *Tribune* wanted a new man, a hero who would reform the city, sweep away the brothels, the intimidators, the mobsters. It proposed a local playboy, William Thompson. As winter turned to cold spring in the windy city, Big Jim need not have worried.

Along with that crowd of elected jokers, they had the sup-port of an Italian immigrant whom they had helped and who in turn was to help them. Big Jim Colosimo was to become as important in the underworld as his Irish predecessor Mike Macdonald, although there is no record that he was ever to make a remark as interesting as one ascribed to Macdonald: when told he was responsible for giving Chicago the title of 'Sin City' he said that he was shocked: he had only committed crime, never a sin. (I suspect that many aphorisms ascribed to

Chicago gangsters were written by men like Ben Hecht or Charles Macarthur, journalists of the golden age.) Colosimo could bring in the Italian vote for the Bath and Hinky Dink, either by blackmailing the customers of his brothels and bars, or by intimidation.

Big Jim had begun his career in the Levee as a street sweeper. His ability to organise fellow workers as a Democratic force had impressed the aldermen. He took the fancy of, and then married, a brothel-owner in the Levee, Victoria de Moresco, and became wealthy. He then intruded upon a sinister activity in the district. For years a group of Italians had been imposing on their fellow immigrants, demanding money on pain of bombing or more particular forms of violence. This was the Black Hand gang. Colosimo, in turn, offered protection against the Black Hand. In passing he offered to hire out destitute immigrants as labourers, finding them work. He seemed a good, strong friend. He followed this success by taking over Black Hand lotteries – later other mobsters and politicians were to take over negro lotteries to advantage. Colosimo had better 'soldiers' than the Black Hand because he was winning. And as his acquaintance with the voters grew so did his friendship with the aldermen.

Colosimo glittered; he was Diamond Jim: a diamond horseshoe on his waistcoat matched those on his fingers and braces. He opened a café on Wabash Avenue, where everyone had to be seen. Enrico Caruso, John McCormack, Galli-Curci, Tetrazzini and the man who had brought all the great singers to Chicago, Campanini, always ate at Colosimo's. Customers would sing; so would waiters. The food, by all accounts, was the best in town and so too the wines. If Caruso and Galli-Curci had known that their host's money was mostly made in the white-slave traffic, his treatment of young girls so revolting as to lead to a change in US law, they would have stayed away. (This was the café that led to the joke in Billy Wilder's *Some Like It Hot*: 'We was all at Rigolettos.') But how could a stranger to Chicago know what was happening when the citizens had small idea?

William Thompson's candidacy and his years in office in Chicago beginning in 1915 are matchless in eccentricity and vulgarity. No Republican before or since ever won so many votes in the city. For a fifteen-year-old minor thief and street-battler like Murray Humphreys, having events interpreted for him by Judge Murray, the 1915 mayoral election must have offered an unforgettable lesson. Here was an incomparable display of language misused in the interests of power, of hypocrisy rampant, of buffoonery exalted, the very stuff of democratic politics. Big Bill Thompson – at forty-eight he was a famous athlete now running to seed – had been a Republican alderman in the city. His family was rich. He had spent much of his life in the West, shooting and drinking. His friends spoke kindly of him: 'The worst you can say about Bill is that he is stupid.' He was a fierce chauvinist, fond of attacking the King of England. If stupid, he had a cunning trait in speaking to the various nationalities which made up his constituency. Among the Irish he would attack the English. Since there was uncertainty about whether the United States would be involved in the World War, he would attack the British or the Germans depending on which part of town he was speaking in.

He would remember, mostly, that he was standing on a platform of reform. He would promise the citizens that saloons would be closed; he would assure the saloon-keepers that they could stay in business. He promised those who were shocked at the amount of gambling in the city that he would crack down on crap-shooting, horse-betting, lotteries and more ingenious methods of removing cash from the voter; he assured the gambling lobby that all was well. 'I'll clean up this city and drive out the crooks. I'll make Chicago the cleanest city in the world,' his peroration would run in his big voice. It was only after he had been elected that he would enliven public meetings by having a local hospital send along a lunatic inmate to appear alongside him on the platform to torment, making out that the sick man was a political opponent (or so Ben Hecht reports).

Thompson becoming mayor was a rare setback for Hinky Dink and the Bath. Their suzerainty of the First Ward, that key constituency in Chicago, Cook County and United States politics, no longer gave them control of City Hall. What would happen to that intricate connection between business, police, gambling and brothels which the Irish and

Italian communities had built up so carefully over nearly half
a century? They could argue, with some justice, that what
they had done was not wholly bad. They had helped poor
immigrants to find a place in a strange, wild land, softened
their hurts and offered them a job or prospects. Indeed, the
English journalist and reformer William T. Stead, if otherwise shocked by the Democratic machine at the turn of the
century, had written with the Bath in mind:

> Here even in this nethermost depth was the principle of
> human service, there was the recognition of human obliga-
> tion, set in motion, no doubt, for party reasons and from a
> desire to control votes rather than to save souls. But what-
> ever might be the motive the result was unmistakable.
> Rough and ready though it may be, the Democratic party
> set in motion an agency for moulding into one the hetero-
> geneous elements of various races, nationalities and religions
> which are gathered together in Chicago.

Certainly Big Bill Thompson's reforming zeal ran quickly
out of breath. Within three months it had become clear to Big
Jim Colosimo that his business could resume. More: in a
development which astonished the Democrats, the Republicans, with the approval of their new mayor, established a
Sportsmen's Club. The annals of sporting life contain libraries
of skulduggery under many titles, from horse-racing through
boxing and, more recently, athletics; this 1915 enterprise in
Chicago races away from the competition. Mayor Thompson
invited subscriptions to the club, the fee being variable and
regular. The committee was soon to consist of Chief of Police
Healey, slot-machine baron Mills and Big Jim Colosimo. This
trio were to make whatever corruption existed before in the
days of Hinky Dink and the Bath seem playful, innocent even,
merely the exuberance of a new society. Big Bill Thompson's
victory on a reform ticket was to have as its consequence an
important reversal of roles between politician and gangster.
Reform meant more power to Colosimo. As John Kobler so
perceptively points out in his biography, *Capone*, whereas
before Thompson's election Colosimo had to go to the Bath
and Hinky Dinky, subsequently these powerful Democrats had

to go to him. They had lost power. Colosimo, by becoming an ally of the mayor's, had gained.

The even tenor or, as reports have it, light baritone of Colosimo's ways was not disturbed by the troubles which beset his friends. In 1917 his fellow-sportsman, Chief of Police Healey, was arrested on multiple charges of graft and bribery. The reform movement had, even after the disappointments of Mayor Thompson, not quite given up. The chief went into the dock with a handful of colleagues and gangsters charged with taking and offering rake-offs from the supposedly-abolished brothels. They were defended by the very lawyer who had so eloquently won the acquittal of Big Bill Haywood in 1907, Clarence Darrow. And they too were acquitted. A great lawyer's gift is as available to the crook as to the hero of the downtrodden, although doubtless his fee was higher for the corrupt cop.

Jim Colosimo by this time, however, like most captains of industry, had acquired a personal assistant. In the nature of things, this was a relative, a New York murderer named Johnny Torrio, who took care of the details. He worked business hours and spent his spare time enjoying music. Like his uncle Big Jim, he was often at the opera. When a murder needed to be arranged he would hire a gun, being both too grand and careful to return to his old trade. Steadily he gathered information about the other gangs in Chicago, learning much which, soon, was to be useful about the Irish boss Dion O'Banion. Torrio was a man happy in his marriage, domesticated, but as cold as death.

Such, in 1919, was the balance between Mayor Thompson and Colosimo, between Republican and Democrat, between law and disorder, when young Murray Humphreys stepped from the Bridewell prison. He was a handsome boy, above middle height and with a head of glorious dark curls, on the threshold of a career more spectacular than he could ever have dreamed of. The forces of good in the United States were about to pass a law which would offer the forces of darkness the chance of mayhem and wealth beyond the imagining of the vice kings and gambling barons. Chicago had seen nothing yet.

5   The arrival of Capone

The moving trigger-finger writes . . .
> F. D. Pasley, after Omar Khayam

Anyone, therefore, who examines the deeds and the life of this man will observe nothing or very little that can be attributed to fortune; since, as was said earlier, not with the aid of others but by rising through the ranks, which involved a thousand hardships and dangers, did he come to rule the principality which he then maintained by many brave and dangerous actions. Still it cannot be called ingenuity (*virtu*) to kill one's fellow citizens, to betray friends, to be without faith, without mercy, without religion; by these means one can acquire power but not glory.
> Niccolò Machiavelli, *The Prince*, 1532

On 17 January 1920 the Eighteenth Amendment to the American Constitution passed into law. This was the Volstead Act. No longer would it be possible to make or sell strong drink in the United States of America. Prohibition, the triumph of the temperance movement, had been a long time a-coming. The evils of liquor were familiar: whisky, bourbon and beer degraded working people and deprived their children of sustenance. In 1848, as the temperance cause gathered puritan strength, Dr Barnes Grindrod had written a polemic – *Bacchus: An Essay on the Nature, Causes, Effects and Cure of Intemperance* – which praised the American Temperance Society for its 'unparalleled exertions in the cause of morals and religion and whose efforts to exterminate the most fruitful source of human misery, the use of intoxicating liquors, will ever ensure them the grateful affections of mankind, and the regard and admiration of posterity.' Eighty-two years later, had such longevity favoured him, Dr Grindrod would have been beside himself with delight. 'It is here at last,' the Anti-Saloon League proclaimed on the eve of Prohibition, 'dry America's first birthday. At one minute past twelve tomorrow morning a new nation will be born. Tonight John Barleycorn makes his last will and testament. Now for an era of clear thinking and clean living. The Anti-Saloon League wishes every man, woman and child a Happy Dry Year.'

The Humphreys family would not have found the success of the temperance movement novel. At home in Wales its triumph may not have been so devastatingly complete but at least it had achieved the Welsh Sunday Closing Act of 1881, an event of some importance since it was the first Act of the British Parliament which applied exclusively to Wales. For nearly a century afterwards it was difficult to buy a drink on the Sabbath. And then, during the First World War, it was the Welsh hero David Lloyd George who imposed on the United Kingdom a law which closed public houses at fixed hours every day. Drink was interfering with the manufacture of munitions.

In the United States the Democratic President Woodrow Wilson had tried to prevent the Volstead Act being passed. He knew his party and, although a former academic, had an understanding of his people. If in matters of international diplomacy he was ignorant and naïve, his insight into the minds of fellow Democrats like Hinky Dink and the Bath was acute. Make illegal a taste people fancy moderately and they will fancy it immoderately. Thus the Bath, at home in the First Ward in the Loop in Chicago, cheerfully, if wickedly, shared the Anti-Saloon League's enthusiasm at a 'new nation' being born. He had laid in, his political insight as fresh as ever, one hundred thousand bottles of bourbon. He sold them immediately at double the price he had paid. Had his commercial gifts matched his political sense he would have held on to them for three years and sold them at ten times the price.

The Bath was not alone in his perception. The Levee may

have gone the way of its flesh. The new phrase was 'the Loop'. Between the skyscrapers of the commercial kings at the heart of Chicago there wound an overhead railway. It looped dramatically and romantically over the heads of the poor and the criminals; alongside stores of rare wealth; past cafés where dazzling talents had fun. Its more excited inhabitants might have it that the Loop encompassed the Florence of the new Renaissance, its more prosaic that there might be a killing to be made; the idiom was never to have more force.

Nowhere else on earth was there such a talent for the mark-up, whether in real estate, girls or dice. Here was a recognition that human frailty is a stuff that, unlike youth, will endure forever. Jim Colosimo, Johnny Torrio and Dion O'Banion slipped like greyhounds from the leash. Had they been more familiar with the history of their Roman church they might have brooded on the unusual state of affairs the Volstead Act had created for the moralist. The Manichean heresy had created difficulty for popes in medieval times. This heresy – which had its origins in fourth-century Persia – held that good and evil were forces of equal power. It is a persuasive thesis. In modern times it has become incredible since the idea that evil exists embarrasses fashionable explanations of human behaviour. Prohibition is an interesting case for the Manichean.

Let us suppose that many of the gangsters were evil men and not, as the phrase goes, victims of broken homes. Here they were in January 1920 witnessing the forces of 'good' – the temperance men and women from the countryside and the puritan enclaves in the wicked cities – delivering into their hands a means of satisfying human weakness, or sin – to wit, booze. History offers nothing to compare: virtue's triumph rewards the worst elements in the society it is attempting to save. Certainly the prohibitionists meant well. Drink and the cynicism of the brewers who produced it were demoralising immigrant communities: Bacchus was not always laughing. Nevertheless good helped evil, although the concept of evil was already vanishing in a society where it was so important to try to believe the best of everyone. Whichever irony beguiled, Chicago was well-placed to satisfy the taste for booze.

Across Lake Michigan lay Canada. Boats could bring in the high-class stuff for the rich. In the city itself thousands of poor people could be persuaded to form an 'alky-cooking' guild making hooch. If they didn't blow themselves up operating the stills, they might blind themselves if they drank the stuff. Many dilutions, many hair-raising or poisonous cocktails were to be brewed in devilish kitchens. To raise a glass was to lend a new nuance to the idea of taking your life in your hand. Any economist of the Chicago school must have been encouraged to see theories of the relationship of price to supply and demand demonstrated so near home.

Consider the astonishment, then, of Johnny Torrio when he discovered that Uncle Big Jim Colosimo began to lose interest in the bootleg trade within months of the bonanza beginning. Here they had a Yukon on their doorstep, a gold-mine that involved little labour beyond hiring murderers and torturers; the mayor was in their pocket; the police were squared; the new morals commissioner had been fired: and all Big Jim wanted to do was to sit making conversation in his café with his friends Caruso and Galli-Curci and dote at home on his new young wife, a serious singer named Dale Winter.

Johnny Torrio did not care for this marriage. Just as Uncle Jim had called him in from the New York mob, so he now recruited from the same gang the young Al Capone. Between them they arranged for Colosimo to be at his café one afternoon to meet some person, unknown to this day. They had appointed a murderer, who went to the café and killed Big Jim. Colosimo was the first of the great gangsters to be murdered at his place of respectable work, setting a precedent for the deaths of O'Banion, Siegel and Giancanna. Only men they trusted could come near enough to kill them, so that each died in whatever unusual comfort the knowledge of treachery offers. Colosimo's funeral also established a precedent.

The Roman Catholic Church refused rites to the gangster on the ground that he was a divorced man, which did not prevent the mob rustling up a Presbyterian minister, nor the Bath from kneeling beside the coffin and reciting such of the Catholic service as he could remember. Five thousand mourners followed the coffin, senators, judges and lawyers mingling with the criminals, among them Johnny Torrio, Al Capone and Dion O'Banion: some $100,000 worth of flowers had been bought from the latter's shop for the occasion. Two brass bands played 'Nearer my God to Thee' and were joined in song by as bizarre a chorus as can ever have been heard in the United States or, indeed, in the history of choral singing. Brueghel or Hieronymus Bosch should have been living in that hour to capture the first flowering of a new, dynamic culture, an assembly of elected representatives of the people, tarts, opera singers, murderers, ponces, law-makers and law-breakers alike, in a multitude of abandoned nationalities and old faiths, united in song: the subconscious of the American dream had broken cover.

There were judges who refused to act as pall-bearers. One was Judge John Lyle, a Republican alderman who resisted Hinky Dink's eloquence. In his *Capone*, John Kobler reports:

> 'Jim wasn't a bad fellow, John,' the Dink pleaded. 'You know what he did? He fixed up an old farmhouse for broken-down prostitutes. They rested up and got back into shape and he never charged them a cent.'
> 'Well,' said Judge Lyle, 'now that he is dead, who's going to run his convalescent camp?'
> 'Oh, Jim sold it. Some of the girls ran away after they got back on their feet. Jim got sore, said they didn't have any gratitude.'

The Chicago *Tribune* the next day reflected that such must have been the homage paid to Caesar, except that here the dead man was overlord of the underworld: 'It is a strange commentary upon our system of law and justice. In how far can power derived from the life of the underworld, influence institutions of law and order?' Others might abide the question, Johnny Torrio had plans. He could not assume that Colosimo's power would be his. He was feared and could walk the streets unarmed. But the Four Deuces bar (so named after the address – 2222 Wabash) where he and Capone were to be found did not have the social appeal of Colosimo's café. No famous opera singer or actor or rich businessman, no socialite, would go near the place although it was only a few yards from the café. This was because the Four Deuces was dark and dirty and because twelve people had been murdered there in twelve months.

Whether Johnny Torrio ever sat down one day and formulated a plan, as Murray Humphreys later was to do in less violent circumstances, no one knows. He was confronting a chaos of crime and corruption of a kind seldom seen before in any nation or city, certainly not for many centuries. Chicago had a score of gangs, their leaders and foot soldiers now forgotten. Each district possessed its hoods, its bombers, its torpedoes. If the Unione Siciliana with its Mafia mode was the most celebrated and profitable, it was only one among many. There was the Polish gang run by Joe Saltis in the stockyards. The fearsome Genna brothers ran the North Side. Roger Tuohy, who was later to play so important a part in Murray Humphreys' life, was powerful on the west of the city. Tuohy's friend, the Jewish crook Hymie Weiss, played a freelance, floating role at this time. Along the waterfront the Irish Dion O'Banion and Bugs Moran held sway. But Torrio and Capone occupied the largest territory to the south. Even while Big Jim was alive Torrio had begun his policy of extending business beyond the heart of the city and Cook County, bribing his way to the creation of gambling dens and brothels in suburbs like Burnham and Cicero.

The gangs were never short of recruits. Children would have their own small groups, usually racial in form. There were hundreds of thousands of poor families in a society in which the emblems of success and manifest wealth were all around; more, one in which material success seemed the only ambition. Two-thirds of the population were either immigrants or the children of immigrants. When it became clear, after three years of Prohibition, that a gangster could enjoy riches without even being especially senior in the mob, an extra incentive was offered the young to join. Away there on the Gold Coast, as the grand houses looking over Lake Michigan were known, there might be, as the Illinois Crime Survey of 1921 observed, 'idealists and reformers'; in the slums the Cadillac came as reward for hi-jacking, murder or a kidnap. The number of recruits increased rather than diminished when the serious shooting began.

Johnny Torrio had tried to avoid mass murder. He had negotiated deals with the various barons, agreeing territories in the manner of Lloyd George, Woodrow Wilson and Clemenceau at the Treaty of Versailles. Alliances would shift, certainly, but for three years violence between mobs was little more than in the decades before Prohibition. After all, some four hundred Italians were murdered in Chicago between 1895 and 1925, all victims of the Black Hand, citizens having no connection with bootlegging, but killed as a result of extortion and blackmail. The murder-standard was unique in Chicago even before the Volstead Act. What helped to spoil any Torrio plan for peace was his development of the liquor trade in such an unexpected style as to transform the profits available and by so doing set alight a forest of jealousy.

Torrio bought breweries. It was, of course, illegal to brew beer, but if those who are duty-bound to enforce a law are inhibited either by being bribed themselves or by knowing their political bosses would not support a prosecution, a law has small or no standing. Thus it was with Torrio's breweries, all five of them. If he was taken to court the fine would be small and business would resume. He became rich beyond the avarice of any earlier princes of the underworld. His power over the speakeasies grew and, incidentally, his influence over the entertainers who sang or played in the saloons. The enduring connection between entertainment and crime in the United States was formed. All this Torrio could not have done without the help of 'respectable' brewers in Chicago who advised him and helped him to arrange the buying of their breweries. These illegal but open alliances were known to many Chicagoans and helped to create the relaxed, often whimsically approving attitude of the city to the mobsters in the Prohibition epoch. His regular sources of supply enabled him to cut prices when it suited him, to discomfit rival beer-runners, a marketing device which did not endear him to enemies. These were forced to depend on quality to defeat Torrio's price policy. But quality was hard to find and so their rivals' response was to intimidate Torrio's customers, hi-jack his trucks and attack his private army which, by 1923, was one hundred strong. His first lieutenant, Al Capone, became restive.

Unlike Johnny Torrio, Al Capone was not a teetotaller (one of the many ironies of the Prohibition period is that Torrio, Dion O'Banion and Murray Humphreys seldom if ever drank). Torrio's efforts to restrain Capone were not especially successful. Thus in 1922 he attracted publicity:

> Alfred Caponi [*sic*]. 25 years old, living at the notorious Four Deuces, a disorderly house at 2222 South Wabash Avenue, will appear in the South Clark Street court today to answer to a charge of assault with an automobile. Early this morning his automobile crashed into a Town taxicab, driven by Fred Krause, 741 Drake Avenue, at North Wabash Avenue and East Randolph Street, injuring the driver. Three men and a woman, who were with Caponi, fled before the arrival of the police. Following the accident Caponi alighted and flourishing a revolver, displayed a special deputy sheriff's badge and threatened to shoot Krause.

The charge was not pursued after a brief appearance by Capone. A very useful precedent was thus set.

Whether – the following May – Capone was carrying his deputy-sheriff's badge when he shot Joe Howard in Heini Jacob's bar a few doors down Wabash from the Four Deuces is not known, but the murder may be taken as raising the temperature in the gang war. The press report the following morning carried a picture of Al Capone, with the brief caption:

> Tony (Scarface) Capone, also known as Al Brown, who killed Joe Howard by firing six shots into his body in the saloon of Heini Jacobs at 2300 South Wabash Avenue, in a renewal of the beer war.

Boiling point was reached on 7 September 1923 and held, to scald Greater Chicago for nearly a decade. The O'Donnell gang, an old-established and old-fashioned Irish group, invaded the saloon of Jacob Geis on West Fifty-First Street. Geis was happy with his supplies from Torrio and Capone and saw no reason to change to those of O'Donnell. He was beaten up. Capone persuaded Torrio that to ignore this treatment of a good customer was bad for business. Therefore the O'Donnells should be pursued. The first of their gang to be shot was Jerry O'Connor; his assassin, a Capone torpedo, was Daniel McFall who was carrying a deputy-sheriff's badge. Wits, with hindsight, were to compare this murder with that of Archduke Ferdinand by Princip at Sarajevo in 1914 and the subsequent gang war with the 'Battle of the Marne'.

Within weeks the tactics of mayhem, soon to become familiar to the world's cinema-goers in the dramatic representations of Capone's life, were on display on street corners, in public buildings, barber shops, brothels and speakeasies, even at the opera house. Capone may have needed a licence to carry a revolver – which he obtained – but his troops, soon to number seven hundred, could buy Thompson sub-machine guns freely since no law existed against their use. This weapon, the tommy-gun, was also known as the 'piano' or 'typewriter'. Bugs Moran, an O'Banionite, developed the technique whereby five limousines, usually Cadillacs, would form a deadly motorcade and drive at speed past their target firing as many as five thousand bullets in a minute. You could always tell, the saying went, when you were near the Capone headquarters in Cicero by the smell of cordite.

Within three months seven of the O'Donnell gang were murdered by the Torrio-Capone faction, some 'taken for a ride' (another new tactic), some shot at the wheel of a bootleg truck; and these were merely the successful shootings. Spike O'Donnell, one of the leaders, was shot at nine times but not once injured. Within three years there were 138 gang killings: 16 in 1924, 46 in 1925, 76 in 1926. Clearly Johnny Torrio's attempt to preserve a system of delineated territory, where each gang could cultivate its garden and supply citizens with the produce they wanted, had broken down. So much so that Torrio decided that a serious gesture was necessary. The Genna, Moran and Weiss gangs were often being difficult, but the most difficult of all was the Dion O'Banion mob. In the public eye the Irishman had come to seem as important as the Italians and if Torrio deplored the Irishman's growing power, Capone envied O'Banion's glamour.

Unlike Capone and Torrio, O'Banion had been born in Chicago. His father was an Irish immigrant in the 1880s, settling in Little Hell, near Death Corner on the North Side. The son became an altar boy at the Holy Name Cathedral, then a newspaper seller and a singing waiter. Murray Humphreys would himself sell papers outside McGovern's Café where O'Banion would sing 'Mary of Argyll' to rowdy delight. By the time of Prohibition the tenor was already a rich gangster and had shot and killed twenty-five people. His florist's on North State Street was one of the most popular in the city, and his gifts to the poor celebrated. Oddly, for one of the most expert marksmen in Chicago, he was an incompetent bank robber. Once he blew out the side of a building while leaving a safe untouched. This was put down to another characteristic: his impatience and reckless-ness. O'Banion smiled when he shot people, and much of the rest of the time too. The Broadway playwright Charles Macarthur, then a journalist in Chicago, used to drive around the lake with O'Banion in the small hours gossiping, and was to ascribe much of his success with women to the flowers O'Banion would give him to offer as presents. When a member of his gang was thrown by a horse as he rode in Lincoln Park, was kicked by the horse and died, O'Banion kidnapped the horse, took it to the park and shot it.

It was his wild mischief which was to be O'Banion's undoing. Not content with two bold pieces of hi-jacking which were the talk of the town – one, seizing $100,000 worth of good whisky from a train in a goods yard and driving it away in lorries, the second driving 1750 barrels of the hard stuff from a warehouse and leaving behind as many barrels of water, police outriders ensuring the safety of the cargo – he decided to annoy Torrio, Capone and the Gennas. His ferocious assistant the Pole Hymie Weiss tried to hold him back, taking the view that he was certain to be murdered. O'Banion would never listen to advice. The Gennas were irritating him. There were six of these Sicilian brothers, senior members of the Chicago branch of the international Unione Siciliana: Angelo, Sam, Jim, Pete,

Tony and Mike. It was O'Banion's opinion that they were invading his territory when there was an agreement that they must not. He complained to Torrio, who did nothing to help. And so O'Banion ordered his men to hi-jack $30,000 worth of Genna's booze. More, he refused to cancel a huge gambling debt of Angelo Genna's even though Johnny Torrio asked him, as a favour, to do so.

He then turned to the matter of Torrio and Capone and invented a drama which struck him as very funny. He would sell Torrio and Capone his share in the Sieblen Brewery for half a million dollars. Torrio agreed, happy to see the back of the Irishman. As if his bootlegging exploits weren't enough, Torrio did not care to see the way in which O'Banion was able to control more votes than himself in Cook County. The hand-over would take place on 19 May. The police arrived simultaneously. Torrio, O'Banion and Weiss were arrested. That nothing came of the charges for a while was neither here nor there. Torrio realised that it had all been O'Banion's idea of a joke. Like the Gennas, he lost patience. O'Banion had said 'to hell with them Sicilians' too often.

The most important Sicilian in town, however, would not allow them to murder O'Banion. This eminent figure was the head of the Unione Siciliana, Mike Merlo, who was O'Banion's only Sicilian friend. Merlo, like Torrio, had been hoping to avoid an outbreak of warfare between the gangs. Torrio and the Gennas had decided in May to rub out O'Banion. On 9 November Mike Merlo died of cancer.

Nearly $100,000 worth of flowers were bought for Merlo's funeral, many of them from O'Banion's shop. His staff had worked through the night. Capone, Torrio and the Gennas had placed expensive orders, one of the latter brothers calling at the shop himself on the day of Merlo's death. At about noon on the tenth a dark Jewett sedan stopped across the street from the shop. Two of the three men who stepped out and into the florist's were described later as Italians, the third as a Greek or a Jew. O'Banion's assistant called him from the back of the shop and he came forward with a carnation in one hand and a pair of flower shears in another. This is taken to mean he knew the men well since with strangers O'Banion always kept one hand free to reach for one of the three guns he carried. The men held him and fired six bullets. The man he knew was said to be a Genna come to buy flowers for Merlo's funeral.

Open warfare began once O'Banion's funeral was over. The Gennas, Capone and Torrio were there, walking behind O'Banion's allies Weiss and Moran. Even the crowds at Colosimo's burial were surpassed. Twenty-six trucks were needed to carry the flowers. Ten thousand marched behind the coffin through streets crowded with thousands more. Another five thousand were waiting at Mount Carmel cemetery. Al Capone held one of his first press conferences to offer his view of the killing of his colleague:

> Deany was alright and he was getting along to begin with better than he had the right to expect. But like everyone else his head got away from his hat. Johnny Torrio had taught O'Banion all he knew and then O'Banion grabbed some of the best guys we had and decided to be the boss of the booze racket in Chicago. What a chance!

The tone of these observations persuaded everyone that it was Torrio or Capone or the Gennas who had shot down the Irishman – as he had shot so many others. O'Banion's allies decided on revenge and that their first victims would be Johnny Torrio and Al Capone.

Torrio left Chicago in fear. While he travelled to Florida and to Cuba – with Weiss's gunmen after him but unable to win a clear sighting – Capone minded a shop which was now producing a turnover of millions of dollars a year. On 12 January 1925, just over a month after O'Banion's murder, Capone's enemies missed him by seconds as he walked into a restaurant on State Street. The death squad fired tommy-guns from a limousine with drawn curtains only three feet from the café entrance. The same day Capone ordered a bullet-proof Cadillac. It weighed seven tons and had windows so arranged as to make firing on the move convenient. Torrio, when he returned to Chicago a few days later, was not so lucky. Weiss and Bugs Moran reached him near his home. They had been waiting there in a Cadillac which Torrio and his bodyguards do not seem to have noticed. The gang leader was shot in the face and chest but as his assailant leaned over him for the decisive shot, found his automatic pistol was empty.

Torrio survived, even chose to go to jail for a year before leaving Chicago, spending some of his fortune in Paris and Naples, and returning to a quiet life in New York. There matters were as peaceful as he had wished them to be in the Windy City. In his former territory the team of Weiss and Moran was making more and more spectacular efforts at revenge. On 20 September 1926 they led an assault on Capone's headquarters on Cicero consisting of eleven automobiles containing some fifty gunmen. The attackers took their time in playing their 'ukeleles' – the fashionable new nickname for tommy-guns. Thousands of bullets smashed windows and doors, almost demolishing the façade. Thirty cars standing in the road were ruined by gunfire. But Capone had fallen to the floor as soon as the shooting started. Indeed the fusillade injured only two people. Hymie Weiss did not long survive this theatrical effort to destroy his rival. Weeks later he was walking past the Holy Name Cathedral, yards from his recently-departed friend Dion O'Banion's flower shop, when assassins in a window shot him down along with his three companions. One of the latter was a lawyer, another a politician.

So brazen a display of public execution was followed by an immediate if unexpected change of tactics. Whether it was the coincidence of these shootings of so many of the gang leaders which prompted his move, or whether some dark plot lay behind it, Capone decided to discover if the gangs could establish a truce, to try to re-create the spirit which prevailed before the O'Banion murder. The principals of the mobs met at the Sherman and drew up a treaty. There was to be an amnesty; the past was forgotten. Territories were to be fixed. The remnants of the O'Banionites would be to the north, Capone to the south, with minor territories for others. And there was to be no more provoking by false gossip, no use of the press to stir trouble. The last devices were known as 'ribbing', which suggests a peculiar sensitivity among semi-literate plug-uglies. With hindsight this agreement has about it a flavour of the later pact between Hitler and Stalin, two men who worked on a larger scale than their Chicago contemporaries but often with similar methods. The pact served Capone's purpose as did the Nazi–Soviet the leaders of nations.

Quite what crimes Murray Humphreys committed in these battles is not clear. While it is said confidently that he killed enemies, had already acquired his expertise in kidnapping, had tossed a few bombs – some of the latter at trucks carrying the bootleg booze of Joe Kennedy, already the father of Jack, the future president – there are no details. According to Murray Humphreys' daughter, Joe Kennedy's men threw bombs at her father. Indeed nearly six decades later, when I held in my hand Murray Humphreys' favourite revolver, observing the three notches on the butt, I thought it reasonable to suppose that these were strikes in the twenties, since he had no need to shoot by his own hand once his authority had been established. However, it was a general rule that in order to demonstrate good faith, loyalty and determination if you were a soldier in a mob, you had to be a torpedo and a pineapple merchant – that is a gunman and bomber.

Neither is it clear, unless this is yet another instance of his insight, why he should have become a soldier for Capone rather than the Irish O'Banion and the Jewish Weiss. Living where he did, near the Loop, he could have chosen to follow a number of leaders. Why then select a predominantly Italian group with Sicilian elements prominent? Given his subsequent career his decision may have been governed by his knowledge of the politics of the Loop and the First Ward from his newspaper-selling days, but this is not quite persuasive since O'Banion and the Irish had, too, a connection with the Bath and Hinky Dink and the other leading Democratic fixers. Whatever his motive beyond mere consanguinity, it was the Torrio-Capone mob he joined and in which after the departure of Johnny Torrio he was soon to rise once the Treaty of the Sherman Hotel was abrogated.

At this point it would be proper to consider the conscience of the murderer, the psychopathology of the torpedo, the hired gun. In most civilised societies killing fellow human beings raises moral questions. Nations have armies and all who have served in them are trained to kill, melodramatic as the concept may seem in retrospect. Quite separate from the matter of the State's authority in ordering citizens to go out and fight, there is the literature of the anguish of the murderer in a cause he believes just: Sean O'Casey's plays are moving examples. However, to raise the question with people in Chicago who have known the prominent gangsters is not fruitful of much discussion. Rather, it puzzles. If you are fighting, you are shooting. The gun becomes the extension of the fist. When, naïvely no doubt, in Chicago I tried to express to Irwin Weiner, a bondsman who had frequently gone bail for Murray Humphreys, how shocked I was that a man had been shot down as he stood next to the bondsman in a hotel car park in 1983 I realised not only that his distress was less then mine might have been, but that the concept was odd.

The responsibility for the general use of arms to settle disputes in the United States is variously allocated. There is that 'frontier' tradition, although the only frontiers the Chicago mobs recognised had nothing to do with open country to the west. There is the Fenian and Sicilian influence. Freudians will have their view, which would extend to the general violence of the society. Wherever the blame is laid there is little sign that the rival armies in the Prohibition battles were much troubled that they shot each other down. Many of the enforcers and ukelele men were psychopaths: O'Banion and Machine Gun Jack McGurk were clearly so, Capone less obviously. With Murray Humphreys the assumption is, as his friend Irwin Weiner suggested, that he had a rough time when young, had to fight, and fell into the habits of the culture. Al Capone once reflected on the moral issue. When one gangster killed another:

> Maybe he thinks that the law of self-defence, the way God looks at it, is a little broader than the lawbooks have it. Maybe it means killing a man who'd kill you if he saw you first. Maybe it means killing a man in defence of your business – the way you make money to take care of your wife and child. You can't blame me for thinking that there's worse fellows in the world than me.

6 Murder into politics

There's one thing worse than a crook and that's a crooked man in a political job. A man who pretends he's enforcing the law and is really making dough out of somebody breaking it, a self-respecting hoodlum hasn't any use for that kind of fellow – he buys them like he'd buy any other article necessary to his trade, but he hates them in his heart.

Al Capone, 5 December 1927

O, Thou that didst care for Nineveh and didst spare it, and Thou that didst weep over Jerusalem, dost Thou still brood over these great modern cities? We pray Thee to rule over Chicago, this young and strong, good and bad city – and out of man's worst to bring Thine own.

The Reverend John Thompson,
Chicago Methodist Temple, 1927

That Murray Humphreys had political interests was first publicly demonstrated on the night of the Illinois State elections in 1930. The date was 4 November. He was thirty years old. Police, searching for Al Capone, broke into the campaign headquarters of Roland V. Libonati who had just won his first election as a state representative. The celebrations at 901 South Halstead Street, Chicago, were rowdy. There was piano-playing and singing. Ten of the company had left their revolvers on top of the piano for safe-keeping. Humphreys' friend Sam Golf-Bag Hunt (so named because that was where he kept his guns) had propped his bag against the piano. The roisterers (Humphreys among them) were taken in for questioning, but soon released. Even fifty-four years later

Mr Libonati, who went on to higher things in the United States Congress, to the dismay of an attorney general in Washington, still spoke with awe of Humphreys. 'His brains brought him power. He was not a man of muscle. He had very high connections.'

Humphreys was already known as Murray the Camel. The nickname had begun as Murray the Hump, after Humphreys, and explicably developed. His closest associates would call him Curly. Only many years later when Capone had gone to jail and 'the Camel' was referred to in the newspapers as 'Chairman of Crime Inc.' and 'Public Enemy Number One', did he acquire fresh sobriquets like 'the brainy hood' or 'the Einstein of the Outfit'.

His introduction into politics, as one of Capone's soldiers, had not been subtle. Little that Capone did was subtle; 'Little Caesar', as he was already known, had been miffed that his friend Mayor Big Bill Thompson had decided not to run for office once more in 1923. A Democrat had been elected, one William Dever, promising to reform the police department. Capone, advised by Torrio, had decided that while it was improbable that any mayor could reform Chicago, it might be as well to take over the government of Cicero – a town, more than a suburb, of some fifty thousand population. His methods were not those Torrio would have recommended.

In the April 1924 elections the all, or non-party group which had ruled Cicero decided that they would break up into Democrat and Republican factions. Capone made a deal with the Republican political boss Vogel that from the mob headquarters at the Hawthorne Inn a campaign would be organised which would guarantee victory: Democrats had best look out for themselves. Vogel's only condition was that Capone should not set up brothels in Cicero. As the Illinois Crime Survey subsequently observed of the election:

> Automobiles filled with gunmen paraded the streets, slugging and kidnapping election workers. Polling places were raided with armed thugs and ballots taken at the point of the gun from the hands of voters waiting to drop them in the box. Voters and workers were kidnapped, taken to Chicago and held prisoner until the polls closed.

A Cicero judge, appealed to by frightened voters on election day, asked Chicago to send help, which came within the hour in the form of seventy special deputies.

Polling ended in a then-unprecedented street battle between the law and Capone's two hundred soldiers, many of whom had been recruited among ruffians for this flowering of the democratic process. Among the gangsters killed was Capone's brother Frank, a prominent murderer: his funeral was held by many to have surpassed Colosimo's in its grandeur. Cicero's elected Mayor Klenha very quickly discovered the character of the political allies who had brought about his big victory.

Within weeks, for all that Mayor Klenha allowed Capone to open one hundred and sixty gambling places in the town, he learned of the gang leader beating up one of his aldermen on the steps of the town hall. Protesting, the mayor was himself beaten up. The mob were now turning over some 3 million a day from enterprises other than bootlegging. They kept the promise not to open brothels in Cicero but compensated by intimidating the authorities in nearby suburbs like Forest View and Berwyn. As Capone observed: 'These are virgin territory for whorehouses.' But this success in Cicero and elsewhere did not satisfy. In Chicago Democratic Mayor Dever was still, if ineffectually, trying to clean up the police and the aldermen. The mob wanted Big Bill Thompson back. They had all the money they needed for a campaign. Would their favourite politician be willing to stand once more in 1927? He would.

For Murray Humphreys this election was in some ways an aberration. The mob were on the Republican side, while his acquaintance was with the Democratic party in the Loop where his future was, most of the time, to lie. However in this mayoral election the criminal element were not divided: all the gangs supported Big Bill Thompson. Capone's enemies, like Moran, and the increasingly bold lesser figures such as the Aieuppas and Jack Zuta – Capone was shortly to kill most of them – also subscribed heavily to campaign funds. If Capone was to claim that he had underwritten the candidature, Zuta boasted that he had been the first to give $250,000 to launch Big Bill on his way. Subsequently there has been confusion between this election and that for Illinois State posts which took place the following year, as to which should properly be known as the Pineapple Election, that is, the one in which many bombs or pineapples were thrown and general thuggery and mayhem obtained. Big Bill Thompson was involved in both. His mayoral election, however, was relatively peaceful, partly because the mobs were united on the Republican ticket. This did not prevent it being one of the more ludicrous ever held in the Windy City.

Big Bill had not abandoned his ability to be all things to all men in his four years out of office. He still placed his faith in the Chicagoans' general indifference to politics and – if not on a pay roll – justified contempt for their local representatives. Thus he let the gangsters know that the city would be wide open once more. The old days would return. 'I'm wetter,' he cried, 'than the middle of the Atlantic Ocean.' However he was against crime:

> The people of Chicago demand an end of the present unprecedented and appalling reign of crime: The chief cause of this condition is not at the bottom, not with the mass of the police department, but it is at the top, with the powers seen and unseen, which rule the force . . . When I was mayor I was held responsible for crime conditions, and properly so, and I accepted that responsibility . . . I drove the crooks out of Chicago, and will do so again if I am elected Mayor.

This ringing lie was immediately followed by the more likely declaration: 'When I am elected we'll not only re-open the saloons these Democrats have closed, but we'll open ten thousand new ones.'

Thompson's campaign song would be sung while the candidate on the platform wrapped himself in the Stars and Stripes:

> America first and last and always!
> Our hearts are loyal, our faith is strong.
> America first and last and always!
> Our shrine and homeland, though right or wrong.

United we stand for God and country,
At no one's command we'll ever be.
America's first and last and always!
Sweet land of freedom and liberty.

Like many a politician in difficulty at home Thompson
turned to foreign affairs. His target was King George V. 'If
you want to keep that old American flag from bowing down
before King George of England, I'm your man . . . It is up to
us, the red-blooded men and women of Chicago, to stand
fast against the pro-British rats who are poisoning the wells
of historical truth.' Of this unusual campaign a wag
remarked: 'Mayor Thompson was for America First and
Capone was for America's thirst.' A contemporary newspaper account of one of his meetings at the Court Theatre
deals with his technique in dealing with opponents (Dr John
Dill Robertson had been a colleague of his but was now standing against him with the help of his former political idol
Fred Lundin):

> Big Bill Thompson put on his rat show yesterday at
> Court Theatre. With two big rats from the stockyards, one
> named Fred, after Fred Lundin and the other Doc, after Dr
> Robertson, the former mayor kept his audience interested
> as he addressed his remarks to the two rodents.
>
> 'This one,' he said, indicating the rat named after Dr
> Robertson, 'this one is Doc. I can tell him because he
> hadn't had a bath in twenty years until we washed him
> yesterday. But we did wash him and he doesn't smell like a
> billy goat any longer.
>
> 'Don't hang your head now Fred,' he said addressing the
> other rat. 'Fred, let me ask you something: wasn't I the
> best friend you ever had? Isn't it true that I came home
> from Honolulu to save you from the penitentiary?'
>
> Big Bill then related how he lived up to the cowboy
> code of standing by his friends and came home as a charac-
> ter witness in the school board graft trial.
>
> Thompson said he had six rats to start with, but said
> that Fred and Doc ate up the other four, which were
> smaller.

On election day there was little more than the usual chicanery of Cook County polling (much the kind of techniques were used which in 1960 were to bring about John F. Kennedy's election as president when all looked lost for him). The important task is to ensure that sympathetic election officials are appointed which, mysteriously, Thompson and Capone were able to do even if, in the normal course of things, this should have been the privilege of the incumbent Democrat. Postal votes will have been acquired beforehand and falsely filled in. Vagrants will have been placed in doss houses and paid to vote the correct way (the 'mattress' vote). 'Repeaters' might vote as many as ten times using a different name and address but knowing that the election officer had been fixed. If these and other dodges failed then there were simple techniques like spoiling ballot papers or throwing them away. It is held that this was the election in which 'vote early and vote often' was coined as electoral advice. The phrase was ascribed to Capone but subsequently was thought to have been one of Murray Humphreys' early witticisms; certainly it is more in his mode of speech than his boss's.

Big Bill Thompson won and there began, in the words of F. D. Pasley who was there at the time and knew many of the protagonists, in 'the Chicago scene of 1927 and the first four months of 1928 – a period so weird that the world sat back and gaped incredulous'. The first event was innocent. Big Bill owned a speakeasy on water, the Fish Fans Club at Belmont Harbour. The night he was elected so many people came to celebrate that the boat sank. No one was drowned. Within the next twelve months nearly a hundred gangsters were to be shot. The Sherman Hotel Treaty was to be forgotten; in its place came the War of the Sicilian Succession.

Capone probably did not want a battle. He was at his zenith. His friend Mayor Thompson turned a blind eye to the bootleggers' trucks which now drove openly through the city. If the mayor's principal assistant Homer K. Galpin would have to leave town because of his involvement with brewers and fixing matters for them, Capone was untroubled. He was expanding his business and had set his colleague Murray the Camel to investigating the possibilities of doing more work in the trade unions and business generally, work for which the impetous and trigger-happy Capone was unsuited. Whether he wanted it or not, however, the Sicilian War came about and was to have far-reaching consequences both for Capone and for Mayor Thompson since what began as insane recklessness had direct political consequences.

The detail of the dispute was not new; indeed its conduct was conventional given that assassination and the rat-tat-tat of automatic weapons had become as much part of Chicago as that new jazz, which Armstrong, Mezzrow, Condon and Beiderbecke were playing in the mobster clubs. The other gangs were jealous of Capone. While rich, making their tens of millions of dollars a year, that Capone made more rankled. Joseph Aiello and his brothers did not care for the fact that Capone had favoured Anthony Lombardo as head of the Unione Siciliana. They made common cause with the equally disaffected Bugs Moran and Jack Zuta. They decided to murder Capone and Lombardo. However, every time they hired assassins, Capone seemed to find out and shot them: Machine Gun Jack McGurk was suspected, rightly, of having this sharp anticipatory sense. When they plotted to poison Capone in a restaurant, the chef shopped them.

In the course of these manoeuvres the police were told that Joseph Aiello was hiding with friends in a house on Washington Boulevard which overlooked Lombardo's house. But all they found hidden were several machine guns which they took to headquarters. The police were then given another address where Aiello might be. He wasn't there either, although they did uncover much dynamite and a note from which they gathered that their man was at the Rex Hotel. And there, finally, they found him and five other hoods, who were taken back to the police headquarters building around the corner from City Hall in the heart of Chicago. There followed the Siege of the Detective Bureau.

Within minutes of the gangsters arriving at headquarters with the detectives, a policeman looking out of the window saw a train of taxis draw up and men run to surround the building. Three of their men entered and one produced a gun. The detective recognised him as a Capone torpedo, later to be prominent and known as Louis 'Little New York'

Campagna. The detective bureau had been surrounded by the Capone gang. The detectives put the three men in a cell next to Aiello and it is reported that Campagna spoke to him in a Sicilian dialect to the effect that Aiello was as good as dead. The newspapers the next day carried banner headlines as ever about Capone's latest dramatic gesture – GUNMEN DEFY POLICE: INVADE LAW'S STRONGHOLD.

Editorials were angry. What kind of city was this, what kind of country was this, where a racketeer could command his troops to surround the citadel of law and order, his gunmen to stroll in armed as casually as if entering a bar? Capone was never more clearly the governor of Chicago and Cook County. The theatricality of the event attracted the world's attention, rather more than did an item which had been fully covered only in the press in Italy, namely that Mayor Thompson had invited Al Capone to be among the official Chicago party to meet Mussolini's friend Commander Francesco de Pinedo, the round-the-world flyer. Chicagoans dismayed at this formal status granted Capone were told, vaguely, that he'd been there in case there had been an anti-fascist demonstration. Was Capone, then, chief of police as well? What other conclusion could be drawn? As ever, neither Capone's insurgents under Little New York nor Aiello were charged after the siege was over.

Capone's rivals were to enjoy the occasional success, but each provoked a fresh slaughter. If they were able to shoot Anthony Lombardo dead on the busiest corner in the United States – on State and Madison – Aiello and brothers and Zuta were to go in response. At which time, suddenly, without any explanation that can be assumed true, Capone decided that he would take a sabbatical. He announced gravely that he was tired of being traduced, that he was merely a businessman like any other providing a service to the public. His motive, his decision to buy a house in Florida among the baroque palaces which Addison Mizner had built for the rich, near those keys where the rum-runners ran, may have been fatigue. He was only thirty years old but his mode of life was not healthy – the rooms full of smoke, the drinking steady, the food heavy, a day at the races not providing much exercise. And a lot of people were being shot; perhaps his luck would run out. Or had he done a deal with Mayor Thompson?

Picking one's way through the political shenanigans of Cook County in this period would tax a commentator brought up in the period of Britain's Tudors or Italy's Borgias. Capone had issued instructions to those enduring old rogues, Hinky Dink and the Bath, that they had to pay him a share of their profits from the gambling pools which had been part of the Democrats' income. Colleagues who harangued Hinky Dink at his craven behaviour in being bullied by Capone were told that he was lucky to have been left any share at all. Are we therefore to assume that the Democrats would, when the time came, have their revenge on Capone and friends? Certainly the Democrats began to move closer to Roger Tuohy, a hitherto unconsidered mobster with Irish connections, and set in process a campaign which was to lead almost to the assassination of President Franklin D. Roosevelt. At the same time the Republicans were about to be divided and so violently that Hinky Dink and the Bath were happy that their heads were low.

A main cause of disturbance on the political – which was to encourage the criminal – front was Mayor Big Bill's belief that he should be Republican President of the United States. He saw a chance on learning that Calvin Coolidge would not seek re-election in 1928. If Coolidge – of whom Wilson Mizner remarked, when that president died, 'How can they tell?' – could be a president, why not Big Bill? Harding had been a Republican president and he, too, had been a crook. And so Big Bill toured the United States offering his patriotic 'America First' arguments. Whether he had told Capone that his cause would not be helped – after the Siege of the Detective Bureau, not to mention the War of the Sicilian Succession – if the Little Caesar was marching through Chicago as if he owned it, is not known. What is certain is that Mayor Thompson set his police on a course of a little light harassment of the mobsters. He then prepared his campaign.

While Capone was away in the early months of 1928, his Outfit was in the hands of his accountant Jake Guzik, more and more advised by his industrial expert Murray the Camel. Thompson, using his mayoral office in the Chicago fashion as

a potent source of patronage, established a team which, as a
first step to the prize in Washington, would contest the Illinois
State elections. No doubt he hoped that the primary election
campaign would be untroubled. Unfortunately for him
Capone's diplomatic absence merely encouraged others to
seize the hour. A minor skirmish among disaffected gambling
bosses led to Capone's friends retaliating by throwing bombs
at the homes of Thompson's 'America First' supporters. A
police guard was needed at Thompson's house.

Chicago's voters were quick to see that the April election
was different in kind from hitherto. Certainly vote-gatherers
had been shot before, but this time the overture was something special. The Senator for Illinois, the Republican
Charles S. Deneen, an enemy of Mayor Thompson's, was to
become involved in a manner he certainly did not seek, but
which was to contribute to an uproar attracting world attention and to an unprecedented number of European journalists
making camp in the city. Part of the reason for the gather-
ing interest lay in the decision by the Federal government to
send agents into Chicago to try to arrest some bootleggers.
Senator Deneen was thought to support these efforts at keeping the law. However, one of the Federal agents shot a
Chicago marshal, the marshal mistakenly thinking the agents
were bootleggers. Chicago's chief of police wanted to arrest
the FBI man who refused to leave the federal building in
Chicago. Mayor Thompson brooded on whether to launch
an attack on the FBI but was somehow dissuaded. Perhaps if
Capone had been in town his decision would have been
different. At which, an ally of Senator Deneen, a man who
was to his Republican faction what Hinky Dink and the Bath
were to the Democrats, Diamond Joe Esposito no less, was
murdered. This popular, if crooked vote-gatherer's assassination was assumed to be the doing of Capone's Outfit.
Mayor Thompson, in a complicated rhetorical flourish, tried
to blame Senator Deneen for the killing, on the ground that
he had introduced the FBI into the city. Such a gesture, the
listener was led to presume, was bound to produce trouble.
For a man aiming for the presidency, Big Bill Thompson was
often puzzlingly given to assuming that Chicago was a
sovereign state.

His arguments persuaded no one. The Outfit was now everywhere in Chicago, beating up Deneen's supporters, bombing their houses and shooting any mobsters who might be against Thompson. The senator's colleagues, often former friends of Thompson's, were belligerent in their eloquence. Edward Litsinger called the Mayor 'a befuddled big beast, low down hound' who had the 'carcass of a rhinoceros and the brain of a baboon'. Some thirty murders were connected with the election campaign. Senator George Norris of Nebraska asked President Coolidge to withdraw US Marines from Nicaragua and send them to Chicago for the primary election. Mayor Thompson could be nautical: 'Bourbon has increased in price from a dollar fifty to fifteen dollars a bottle and King George V's rum-running fleet, eight hundred miles long, lies twelve miles off our coast, so every time you take a drink you say, "Here's to the King".' The European journalists had not wasted time in seeing the election as a rich piece of Americana.

In the last weeks of the election campaign the churches in the city began to offer up prayers. One Sunday, worshippers in five hundred churches of all denominations – one report has it there were one hundred thousand voices as one – asked that 'the city might be delivered of graft and corruption at the April primaries'. The next day the house of Senator Deneen was bombed. However, prayers for a large registration of Republican voters were answered, even though Diamond Joe had gone to that bourne where no votes are fixed. If these manifestations of unusual public interest dismayed Mayor Thompson he showed no outward sign. Wrapped once more in his Stars and Stripes he would bellow out his new song with his entertained audiences:

Scanning history's pages, we find names we love so well,
Heroes of the ages – Of their deeds we love to tell,
But right beside them soon there will be a name
Of some one we all acclaim.
Who is the one, Chicago's greatest son?
It's Big Bill the Builder.
Who fought night and day to build the waterway.
It's Big Bill the Builder.

59

To stem the flood, he stood in mud and fought for all he's
   worth;
He'll fight so we can always be the grandest land on earth;
He's big, real and true – a man clear through and through –
Big Bill the Builder – We're building with you.

Al Capone returned to Chicago to supervise the polling.
Senator Deneen's faction, standing on an anti-crime ticket,
had its own gangs but they were outnumbered and lacked the
firepower of Little Caesar's army. Plastered with 'America
First' stickers the curtained limousines with tommy-guns
poised, the black Cadillacs and the chief's armoured car
gathered at the Hotel Metropole headquarters. Here Capone,
confident since Mayor Thompson's victory in 1927, had a
suite of fifty rooms. Usually it was crowded with city hall
people, lawyers, judges and policemen passing the time
of day, collecting their rewards. In April 1928 his thugs
gathered for instructions, to learn fresh refinements on the
way in which an election should be handled. The message
was plain. If they could not persuade voters to support
Mayor Thompson's slate, they were to ensure that they did
not vote against him, and to that end they were to use their
guns, and their bombs, or at least slug people.
   The gun and the bomb distinguished the tactics, were
added sanctions to normal conduct. Thus if a citizen was
voting frequently and an electoral officer objected, a Capone
soldier would pull a gun on him. If an officer protested
when a gangster brought into a booth a heap of ballot
papers marked for Thompson he would be kidnapped,
Capone informed, and a replacement be sent from the pool
of Thompsonites the gangster had with him at the Hotel
Metropole. Thugs would call at houses and if they discovered anyone unwise enough to say they supported
Senator Deneen's cause, they would either thump them
or threaten to bomb the house. From time to time Capone's
mob and Deneen's hoods would exchange fire in the streets.
One candidate on the ticket, a Negro, was shot and killed
by a passing Capone platoon. In the enquiry which followed the election – a normal event in Chicago – it was
discovered that one voter had appeared in sixteen polling

stations always giving the same address, that of a riding stable: 'Every horse voted,' as a wit had it.

The understanding was universal that Thompson's men must win in an electorate so intimidated. The astonishment proved equally universal when it became clear that in the votes which mattered they had lost by a margin of two to one. For once the citizens had bothered to turn out and declare that they did not want Al Capone running their city. He simply did not have enough soldiers to bomb and shoot and defraud on the necessary scale. Throughout the United States and Europe the response to the result, to the defeat of Thompson and Capone, varied from the patronising to the ecstatic. 'There is a God in Israel,' declaimed the *Kansas City Star*, from a city which could have used a minor deity itself. 'The objection to having Chicago elections dominated by bombs and its everyday affairs superintended by gunmen with machine guns was an important factor in the election,' wrote the *San Francisco Chronicle* in an appraisal which can scarcely have taken its readers aback. The London *Daily Telegraph* believed that 'a miracle had supervened'. Indeed there was a general belief that the future would be different in Chicago now that citizens had expressed themselves. However there were gangsters and politicians who interpreted the result differently, Murray Humphreys among them. Capone did not propose to change his ways as his Outfit was to show within nine months of the Pineapple Primary when it carried out the most brutal and celebrated of all its murders.

7   The St Valentine Day Massacre

Wherefore it is to be noted that in taking a state its con-
queror should weigh all the harmful things he must do and
do them all at once so as not to have to repeat them every
day, and in not repeating them to be able to make men feel
secure and win them over with the benefits he bestows on
them. Anyone who does otherwise, either out of timidity
or because of poor advice, is always obliged to keep his
knife in his hand; nor can he ever count upon his subjects,
who because of their fresh and continual injuries, cannot
feel secure with him. Injuries therefore should be inflicted
all at the same time, for the less they are tasted, the less
they offend; and benefits should be distributed a bit at a
time in order that they may be savoured fully.

Niccolò Machiavelli, *The Prince*, 1532

Quite what process it is in the human imagination which
makes one event universally memorable while another of the
same kind of far greater import remains ignored, is impossible to explain. Consider separate bursts of machine-gun fire
on St Valentine's Day, the one in 1929, the other in 1933. In
the first, seven gangsters are murdered in a garage in Chicago
by other gangsters, a commonplace in that city at that time.
In the second, hundreds of workers are shot by the troops
of the fascist Heimwehr in a battle in Vienna between the
government and the socialists which the perceptive could
recognise as presaging the Second World War. Few recall the
tragedy of the Austrian capital; everyone knows about the St
Valentine Day Massacre. The Chicago murders, it is true,
have been represented in many films. Billy Wilder's *Some*

Like It Hot offered a comic version. Perhaps the image is enduring because it encapsulates an epoch in American life as a painting or a novel might another society's distinctive days. What happened, to Hitler's and Stalin's delight, in Vienna on St Valentine's Day, was complicated and in a foreign language and there were no famous movies.

Although it was said years later that Murray Humphreys was involved in the organisation of the massacre, often by people who gossiped in the underworld, there is no direct evidence that the police interrogated him. That may not prove anything, either. The elements in the crime which suggest that he was involved are first the fact that Al Capone was actually in the office of the Miami chief of police while the massacre was taking place, a coincidence which has the mark of the Camel's sense of humour. Secondly, one of the men murdered was a speakeasy owner whom Humphreys was keen to see the end of since he was a direct rival in the protection rackets, a department of crime which the Welshman had now mastered on behalf of his boss. This foe was Al Weinshank, a member of Bugs Moran's gang. Wasn't it strange, too, that the massacre took place just twenty yards from the house in which the Camel had been born? And later he used to call the building in which the Outfit met 'Schneiders', as if after the family which had overheard the shots being fired on St Valentine's Day? That may just have been his sense of humour, too.

The object of the exercise was to kill Bugs Moran and as many of his associates as possible to demonstrate that the Capone mob was in charge. Moran was suspected of hi-jacking, or buying from hi-jackers, Capone's supplies of a popular brand of whisky, Old Log Cabin. To test this theory Moran's confidence was built-up in a dealer, a supposed hi-jacker. This double agent, now trusted by Moran, told Moran to expect a consignment at the garage in North Clark Street at 10.30 in the morning of 14 February. Two of Capone's men were overlooking the scene from a house across the street. Punctually most of the members of Moran's gang arrived, the Gusenberg brothers Frank and Pete, Adam Heyer, James Clark, Reinhardt Schwimmer, who was not actually a member but an amateur observer of low life, and

Al Weinshank. Also there was a mechanic, Johnny May, who had his German shepherd dog Highball with him, his leash tied to a truck. Bugs Moran, Ted Newberry and Willie Marks were late, and were to offer a useful argument against any merit in being punctual for a business appointment.

It can be very cold in Chicago and the wind blows down North Clark Street: I once had my vocal cords freeze whilst standing and staring at a building where Moran's garage had stood. (Rumour has it that many citizens have pieces of the place as souvenirs.) On the day of the notorious gunfire, snow was falling. A police car came down the street, once known to the Indians as the Green Bay Trail. In front sat two uniformed men, behind were three civilians. This was a genuine police car, no phoney mock-up. It had curtains and a gong. But at a signal from the Caponeites in the window across the street the car pulled up at the garage entrance. This was the only error Capone's men made. The signal was to mean that Bugs Moran was inside. He was not. Al Weinshank had been mistaken for him, being of much the same build and wearing a tan fedora of the kind Moran favoured. Moran and Newberry, a few minutes late, saw the police car outside the garage, assumed they had been betrayed by someone, didn't worry too much and went away.

Inside the garage the two Caponeites dressed as policemen took weapons from the gang and made them stand facing the wall. The room, by all accounts, was bleak, the temperature well below freezing, lit by a single, bare 200-watt lamp. The three men who had been sitting in the back of the police car now entered, one carrying a tommy-gun, the others shotguns. The firing lasted a minute, making a dreadful racket heard around the neighbourhood. Then silence, except for Highball's howling. A lodger in an apartment nearby saw the three men leave the garage with two policemen behind them pointing guns at their backs, and assumed there had been a battle with the forces of law and order. Bravely – his name was McAllister – he went into the garage. One of the seven men was still alive: Frank Gusenberg. He was asked who had shot him. 'Nobody shot me,' he replied. He had fourteen 45-calibre bullets in his body. When Bugs Moran was given the news he said: 'Only Capone kills like that!' When Al Capone was told in Miami in the warm winter sun he said: 'Only Bugs Moran kills like that.'

Coming so swiftly on the heels of the Pineapple Election with its promise of a change of city habits, the massacre assured the world and the citizens of Chicago that Capone's power remained intact. The scale, brutality and expertise of the shooting awed. The crime carried another doubt into the public mind: could those men dressed as policemen have been real policemen? It was not a wild surmise, yet the cynicism was misplaced. The police tried very hard to make arrests. Machine Gun Jack was taken in and various other hoods, but no charges could be made to hold. As it happened all the suspects were soon to be killed by fellow gangsters in subsequent battles, a swiftness of justice which the normal processes of law would not have achieved.

For Murray Humphreys the massacre was particularly helpful since Weinshank had gone. His death emphasises a neglected aspect of the shooting. Because it was about hi-jacking a load of whisky it has reasonably been seen as the consummation of gang warfare in Chicago. Weinshank's presence offers a different perspective since he had only been a member of Bugs Moran's gang for a few weeks. His speciality was trade union and industrial affairs, as the Camel's had become. His presence in the most brutal and reckless of all the evil plots conjured up by the principal hoods graphically illustrates the horrors of the gang's presence in the working and business life of Chicago. That civic conspiracy whereby the torpedoes and thugs were taken tolerantly because they were providing people with booze wears thinner if behaviour separate from the operation of the Volstead Act is considered. Under cover of the power of bootlegging the mobs had begun to diversify well beyond their traditional exploiting of human frailty in gambling and prostitution.

'Rackets' had grown up with Chicago and took amazing forms. Technically, a bootlegger was not a 'racketeer' although he might become one as the result of his illegal business. The proper racketeer was someone who might be a union organiser, or the boss of a business which appeared legitimate, or he might be a thug. In 1927 the Chicago *Journal of Commerce* writing, surely, from the heart, expanded on the word's local connotation.

> Whether he is a gunman who has imposed himself upon some union as its leader, or whether he is a business association organiser, his methods are the same; by throwing a few bricks into a few windows, an incidental and perhaps accidental murder, he succeeds in organising a group of small business men into what he calls a protective association. He then proceeds to collect what fees and dues he likes, to impose what fines suit him, regulates prices and hours of work, and in various ways undertakes to boss the outfit to his own profit. Any merchant who doesn't come in or who comes in and doesn't stay in and continue to pay tribute, is bombed, slugged or otherwise intimidated.

As early in his career as 1922 Murray Humphreys, according to the testimony of the Chicago Commissioner Virgil W. Peterson to the US Senate in 1950, had tried to move in on the milk-drivers' union. He proposed an ingenious scheme: the union should amalgamate with the janitors' union. Together they would approach the owners or tenants of tenement blocks and tell them they wouldn't have any milk delivered unless more janitors were employed, or wages were increased. This plan was to work later. Another gambit was to extort money from people living high in skyscrapers and tell them that if they didn't pay up, the lifts would keep stopping lower down. This was successful. But these were minor episodes compared with Humphreys' exploits once he had become Capone's principal in the rackets.

At the time of the St Valentine Day Massacre the Illinois attorney's office calculated that there were nearly a hundred business associations or trade unions run by racketeers. Master Photo Finishers, the Motion Picture Operators (which the Camel was later to use for one of his most spectacular *coups*), the City Hall Clerks, the Painters and Decorators, the Jewish Chicken Killers, the Glaziers, the Musicians, the Retail Food and Fruit Dealers were just a handful of them. The case of the Master Cleaners and Dyers

Association and the Sanitary Cleaning Shops shows that Murray Humphreys by 1928 had become the master of the rackets. His style is established, his technique polished already to that mixture of charm and ruthlessness, insouciance and brutality which was to impress gangster, politician, lawyer and FBI alike throughout his career, and to enrage Attorney General Robert Kennedy in the late fifties and early sixties.

The principal dyer and cleaner in Chicago was Morris Becker. Over forty-two years he had built his business into ten large establishments distributed throughout the city. In 1928 he claimed that the Master Cleaners and Dyers Association wanted to control cleaning. They wanted to dictate prices to him. 'My places have been bombed time and time again; my employees slugged, robbed and threatened; then without warning they were called out on strike. Union officials told me I would have to see Walter Crowley, manager of the Master Cleaners. Crowley said if I paid $5000 and joined the Association everything would be okay.' He refused to have anything to do with them. He was next approached by more senior gangsters Rubin and Abrams. They told Morris Becker that there was going to be a price rise of from 40 to 50 per cent in cleaning clothes. He again refused, at which he was told he was going to be bumped off. Courageously he took the association to court where, once more, Clarence Darrow defended the monopolists, or extortioners, successfully. At which Becker turned to Capone and Capone turned to Humphreys.

Humphreys had already appraised the situation and had somehow acquired a laundry business. He met Becker and five other like-minded owners. He advised them to form a new group, which they did. Among the shareholders in the Sanitary Cleaning Shops were Al Capone and his faithful accountant Jake Guzik. The new organisation employed Humphreys to act as an 'arbiter' in labour disputes. He was also to use his influence to discourage the manipulation of prices, whether increases or price-cutting. He was to be employed for a year at a salary of $10,000. Immediately he settled the strike which had been plaguing Morris Becker and he 'persuaded' the Master Cleaners and Dyers Association to

forget about raising prices. INDEPENDENT CLEANERS BOAST
GANGSTERS WILL PROTECT WHERE POLICE FAILED, ran one
headline. This episode won Capone some credit. Humphreys
modestly stayed in the background but his triumph had an
important effect in the racketeering world. He became a kind
of consultant to the underworld and that half-world in which
so much of Chicago's business, especially its public business,
operated. How had he managed it?

Humphreys had moved in on Local 46 of the Laundry,
Cleaning and Dye House Workers International Union –
indeed was to remain in control until his death in 1965. Since
he was representing Capone he could frighten anyone. At the
same time he used his position as an owner to threaten force
against the association. He was thus in a unique position to
arbitrate since he was representing both sides. Inevitably the
triumph was brief. Soon Al Weinshank appeared on the scene
to fight back for the discomfited association and since the
Camel had Capone's backing, in turn he went to Bugs
Moran. If, on the booze front, the relationship between
Moran and Capone was held to be good, in the legitimate
laundry business the war was fierce. Humphreys stationed his
troops in a dry-cleaning plant on the South Side, Weinshank
on the North Side. It was a spectacular and nasty contest,
larger in scale – though not in kind – from others which were
the consequence of racketeering.

Humphreys' opponents were not without ingenuity. One
of their tricks was to place inflammable chemicals in a suit
and send it to a rival cleaner's. It would blow up. Humphreys
relied more on acid-throwing and bombing. In the course of
the conflict five people were murdered and many battered.
Thirty laundries were bombed and as many damaged by
acid. While not attracting the attention of the War of the
Sicilian Succession this racketeering touched more nearly the
working life of the people of Chicago and in the long run, as
Humphreys perfected his trade, had a more enduring effect
on the country. Of course, the people who had employed
Murray Humphreys, men like Morris Becker whom the
police could not help, who meant and hoped well, found when
his year's employment was up that suddenly Humphreys
wanted very much more money. Shall we say 30 per cent of

the profits? Or else? At which point, by sweet chance, his enemy Al Weinshank is shot down in the St Valentine Day Massacre.

Humphreys was never to look back, as the phrase goes, but especially with meaning in his case with so much to be uneasy about. His reputation was assured. Whether or not it was the laundry's influence, he became at this time celebrated for the elegance of his clothes. He wore his straw hat in summer. Unlike his vulgar comrades he smiled easily and joked, as well he might because he suddenly saw an opportunity in the death of Weinshank which he was quickly to seize. Small wonder that there is a suspicion he might have had a hand in the St Valentine Day Massacre.

8 A change of strategy

Murray 'the Camel' Humphreys and Frank 'the Enforcer' Nitti are ready to surrender. They have had enough of the blood-letting. 'Too many of our friends are being killed.'
Chicago *Daily News*, 17 December 1932

And thus anyone who does not diagnose the ills when they arise in a principality is not really wise; and this skill is given to few men. And if the primary cause of the downfall of the Roman Empire is examined, one will find it to be only when the Goths began to be hired as mercenaries; because from that beginning the strength of the Roman Empire began to be weakened, and all that strength was drained from it and was given to the Goths. I conclude, therefore, that without having one's own soldiers no principality is safe; on the contrary, it is completely subject to fortune, not having the power and loyalty to defend it in times of adversity. And it was always the opinion and belief of wise men that 'nothing is so unhealthy or unstable as the reputation for power that is not based on one's own power'.
Niccolò Machiavelli, *The Prince*, 1532

Murray Humphrey's practical duties were made much easier than they might otherwise have been for two reasons. First, Weinshank (months before he was shot down on St Valentine's Day) and Moran had recently murdered two of the most important labour figures in the city, John Clay and the Irish Tim Murphy. Rivals had thus been removed without troubling the Camel. Clay was shot because he was honest,

70

Murphy because he was a crook who didn't care to do a deal with Weinshank. Murphy's death was important since he was the boss of the building workers and in cahoots with employers and City Hall. He was expert at demolishing the buildings of the unco-operative. He liked Catholic priests to appear on public platforms with him. In 1922 fourteen buildings had been blown up with Murphy's help. Since he was also boss of the Street Sweepers' Union, following in the path of Big Jim Colosimo, he could then lend further help in clearing up the mess.

The second reason was that the Camel was the most practised and successful of kidnappers and so found no difficulty in moving from the relatively frivolous practice of his trade in the bootlegging field to its more serious employment in industrial affairs. Among the bootlegging gangs, to be kidnapped was a mild form of threat or, at most, a nuisance if it was to lead to a truck of booze not being picked up. The sums demanded for ransom were small although not so minute as to be an insult to a mobster's standing. In the business and union field the practice was now brutal, now devious, and brought the Camel public attention. When in 1930 the Chicago Crime Commission, searching helplessly to bring sense into affairs, decided to name leading gangsters as Public Enemies, Al Capone became Number One and Humphreys Number Two. Who was this Humphreys? Where had he come from? The press published a picture of him wearing his straw hat. He didn't look like all the others. How could a Welshman be a gangster, a gangster a Welshman? Curiosity was not satisfied. The Camel was elusive – to journalists, as to historians, as to the law.

In the case of Benjamin Rosenberg, a laundry owner who resisted Humphreys' agents to the point of appearing before a grand jury and testifying against his intimidators, there was a possibility that the Camel might appear in court. Rosenberg was murdered before the case could proceed. The prosecution threw up its hands. When Dennis Zeigler of the Housing and Portable Engineers Union was kidnapped and murdered, Humphreys was arrested but immediately released when it became clear that he was far away and busy when the crime was committed. Years later a gangster charged for a murder elsewhere mentioned in passing, during his trial, that he had been present in a restaurant in Chicago in 1929 when he had seen the Camel shoot a man and ask the assembled company if they would mind helping him to lift the body into a back alley. Humphreys responded by observing that no one was ever killed in Chicago after 1929 without himself being bothered by enquiries. The more general view, expressed by politicians, federal agents and mobsters, was that Humphreys by the time of the Massacre had become too grand to kill. However, it is the case that different authorities place the year his apprenticeship ended variously from 1928 to 1933. Since he was a wealthy man from 1928 onwards it does seem unlikely that, given the forces he could hire, he would need to do any dirty work for himself. Especially since he had just married a girl from Oklahoma and was settling down to domestic life, one different from the style of his Sicilian and Irish colleagues.

Humphrey's success in this period was remarkable. Some 70 per cent of the rackets in Chicago came under the control of men responsible to him, producing an income of $80 million a year. That cash led to workers earning lower wages than they might have, to prices for most goods and food being higher than they might otherwise have been, to fear and trouble extra to the normal anguish of life in a great city being imposed on anyone hoping to make a living in a small business. However, his power still depended on his being Capone's man. But Capone was running into a storm which was to destroy him.

On the face of it, Capone looked secure. He had an income of $40 million a year and if he lost a fifth of it in gambling – he was probably the unluckiest or worst gambler ever known – had he not achieved the Chicago dream? To be rich and out of jail? He had succeeded in calling a conference of gangsters from throughout the United States to set up a cartel of the kind respectable industry always aimed at, but in this case a brotherhood of crime. Capone was not a Sicilian himself and so could not head the Unione Siciliana or Mafia. This did not trouble him since he enjoyed a superior power: he could murder a president of the Mafia, like Frank Yule. He could grant an audience to an enrapt world's press. In polls throughout the nation he was high on any list of the most famous Americans. But in 1931, as he put it, people started ganging up on him.

To begin with, there was no prospect of Big Bill Thompson winning re-election as mayor. A low-down Democrat ward-heeler, Anton Cermak, was running for the Democrats and likely to win. And there were these federal men breaking into his offices and asking about his income. They had tested the ice by charging one of his brothers for income-tax evasion and winning a conviction. The Little Caesar was to be next. Strangely – or probably not, given the moralities of the United States – a failure to pay tax was to be Capone's downfall. The slaughter he had caused, the corruption he had heightened, the terror he had brought into Chicagoans' lives, the enduring image he had created of America, all this could have brought him a benign old age. But he had not paid his income tax. Even here the nonsense does not end. Capone and his friends properly pointed out that J. Pierpont Morgan, perhaps the richest man in the world, a man whose agents had caused mayhem among strikers, paid no federal income tax at all between 1929 and 1932. The proprietor of the *Chicago Tribune*, Colonel Robert McCormick, a multi-millionaire, chose to value his property in Chicago at $25,000 and pay tax of $1500. The voices of those who thought other people apart from Little Caesar might be indicted were not much heard from.

While these trials were beginning for Capone – and soon his faithful accountant Jake Guzik was to be arraigned on a similar charge – Big Bill Thompson was being replaced as mayor by Anton Cermak. Thompson had never recovered from the rebuff of the Pineapple Primary and the crimes which followed. The Democratic machine had begun to function again under the leadership of Cermak, an old hand. Once more the campaign had been conducted on the promise to clear the gangsters out of Chicago. Cermak was for honest government. He would drive Capone out of town. And certainly it began to look as if he meant business. In no time at all ninety Capone soldiers were killed in battles, ambushed, confronted with police in unreasonable betrayals. Was this because Capone was away? Because Guzik was occupied in fighting tax charges? At headquarters Humphreys and his colleague Frank 'the Enforcer' Nitti were troubled. Humphreys had a mind to give to the difficulties – already he had been graced with City Hall's compliment that he was the 'brains' of the Outfit. Nitti did not have much of a mind, especially since a city officer had just walked into the Outfit's headquarters and shot him in the head. (Later it was to emerge that the policeman shot an unarmed Nitti in the interests of a gambling deal which the new reforming Mayor Cermak had done. The court case became one of Nitti prosecuting the policeman who kept mum on the mayor's orders.)

Given that Humphreys was working in a state of confusion among the gangs and with little political intelligence, his course of action shows an acute intuition. Because Capone had supported the Republican Mayor Big Bill Thompson, relations with the Democratic party were bad. Capone had been unpleasant to Hinky Dink and the Bath and their friends. Humphreys knew enough of ward politics to realise that Anton Cermak could not mean that he intended to put an end to the gangs. Therefore – it is not easy to empathise with the Camel in his predicament but given his subsequent style not impossible to guess at it – the new mayor must mean that he intended to support a gang other than Capone's. In this judgment Humphreys was largely correct. There is a possibility, though, that Cermak had evolved a more sophisticated plot, that he had in mind to make his City Hall the gang itself, that he would actually formalise crime in government. This would make even deeper the hypocrisy the mayor exhibited as he stood alongside Franklin D. Roosevelt at the latter's nomination in Chicago for the presidency and listened to the eloquent promulgator of a New Deal for America, to his assault on the 'malefactors of great wealth' and win support for his victorious campaign for the White House.

The next time Mayor Cermak stood alongside President Roosevelt he was shot and was to be dead within three weeks, a melodramatic event in Florida in 1933 which exemplifies, in the complexity of its motives, the problems Humphreys had been confronted with in Chicago. He had concluded that the mayor was supporting Roger 'the Terrible' Tuohy's gang, an unconsidered Cook County mob of bootleggers. There was no other explanation of the way in which apparently unaffiliated torpedoes were shooting Capone's men. There was growing evidence that Democrats were busy among the speakeasies and particularly the gambling 'wheels', taking their percentage and telling the hucksters that they could look to City Hall for protection against City Hall and Capone's men. The police, that is, would be winning their rake-off not from Capone but from within the political structure. If Cermak's policy was perfect corruption, a corruption so pure that it requires no racketeers or crooks, where had he learned such philosophical clarity?

Anton Cermak had been a coal-miner. He had come young from Bohemia (later to be part of Czechoslovakia), and thus was, like Humphreys, not a part of the Irish or Italian or Sicilian groups from which the mobsters sprang. Sensibly he allied himself with the Irish faction led by Hinky Dink so that he was thought one of them and became an industrious vote-fixer and an opponent of Prohibition. He was not a gangster; he never killed; yet he used a gangster – Tuohy – to help him to create probably the most corrupt government machine Chicago had seen, one that was to be inherited after his assassination by the Democrat Kelly-Nash partnership in City Hall, to serve as a model for the criminal political mind. Why should this be so? Why should Chicago nurture such ambitions above other cities?

The problem has been confronted more or less directly by many thinkers. One explanation is that commerce and crime are merely two sides of a coin. When gold is worshipped morality is irrelevant. However, there were immigrants in Chicago, millions of them, who did not nurture mobsters and racketeers: Swedes, English, Germans, Greeks, hardly a soul involved. In *The Bootleggers* the British writer Kenneth Allsop considers the question. He writes that the Irish, Sicilians and Jews were the principal villains. In fact, there were very few Jews in the mobs. However, Allsop's thesis is:

The Irish, the Sicilians and the Jews had one experience in common that the other racial-groups had not: European backgrounds in which self-preservation had depended upon fighting and clannish solidarity against an internal enemy – the English land-owners and soldiery in Ireland, the French occupation forces in Sicily, and the antiSemitism that ringed the Jews in almost every European city. The ancestors of the Prohibition gangsters had survived by using their muscles and their cunning. Their parents came over to America with an ingrained bitter antipathy towards the theory of justice, which, in their experience was more often than not used as a truncheon of despotism, and consequently they were not so easily dazzled and drawn by the American lodestar of middle-class managerial respectability.

If there is little reason to place the Jews in the same context as the Irish and Sicilians there remains a common factor between the latter which Allsop skirts: the Irish and the Sicilians and Italians like Capone were Roman Catholics. Certainly they had felt oppressed at home. Yet other people in other European states had known the heel of the landlord or the alien prince and had not become gangsters in Chicago or elsewhere in America. Many Protestants or religiously indifferent immigrants led earnest and virtuous lives. Indeed most Catholics did. They wished to create a new, free society in which they could prosper. However, it is the case that most hoodlums were Catholic and so were most of the politicians who conspired with them.

Observers of the development of crime and its relationship with the State in America are reluctant to make much of this preponderance of one faith. If sex was a taboo subject in the nineteenth century and death in the latter part of the twentieth, to ascribe behaviour to the citizen's religion smacks in both epochs of a peculiarly bilious form of prejudice, one even worse than racialism. No one would suggest that a gangster was so because he was a Catholic. Why, though, should crime be so much associated with the Roman version of Christianity?

Many a Protestant would suggest – has suggested – that the nature of Catholicism presents the sinner with an easy escape in this world. The confessional exculpates. The conscience does not trouble the criminal since he regards himself as serving a power higher than himself. His behaviour is not truly his responsibility. Morality is the concern of the priest. This reading would offend the truly religious, perhaps: it was the common understanding of the illiterate layman. Murray Humphreys was to discover in the forties, when it mattered, that it was not difficult to find priests to testify to the sterling worth of fellow hoods who were anxious to be paroled from the cooler. He probably recalled, being a Protestant himself, that it was Big Jim Colosimo's divorce rather than his murderous conduct of his brothels which made the Roman Church refuse to take the gangster to its bosom at the death. There were, too, other characteristics of Sicilian and Irish society, related to their faith, which encouraged the mobsters. After all, if their common trait was that their nations had been oppressed, why was each group quite so quick to fight amongst themselves in Chicago, to oppress each other?

When a community has its faith taken care of, it then looks after itself. Politics becomes a matter of looking after your own. Objective standards, the pursuit of justice: all that is put to one side. Spiritual questions have nothing to do with who has this job or that, this contract or that; the politician who doesn't line his pocket is regarded with suspicion: what can he be up to? Those familiar with Irish or Sicilian politics long after the oppressor nation has vanished will recognise the portrait of such a community. The loyalty to the family supervenes on a loyalty to a state or any community removed from the family. Historians have proposed that the development of British cities like Liverpool and Glasgow changed in character not exclusively because their imperial role was lost, but because Irish immigration replaced the Protestant ascendancy with a Catholic. Therefore the connection between Chicago and these once formidable European ports from which so many migrants sailed to America was more than a sailing of heavy-laden ships. The shadow of the gunman also lay over the Irish capital Dublin as it does still over Belfast and Sicily.

Finding himself, a Protestant, suddenly having to solve immediate difficulties for troubled troops of different nationality and faith, Humphreys is reported to have been near despair. Or was it that he wished it to be thought so? Certainly it was a desperate position to be in. The chief of police called him in and told him he was finished. The problems were not only within the gang. America itself seemed to be crumbling in a Great Depression. No city in America suffered higher unemployment than Chicago. In one month in 1932 thirty-eight of its banks went bust. The gangsters found a wry comfort in seeing the bankruptcy of Chicago financiers who for so long had been paraded as the good men around the place, men like Charles T. Yerkes and Samuel Insull. Many other Chicagoans found that Insull and Yerkes were more disgraceful than Capone and friends since they had stolen even more money, been more brutal in their price-fixing, more corrupt even in their political dealings. (And not even been amusing like, say, a fine fraudster and stock-waterer in New York, Jim Fisk, who was 'first in war, first in peace and first in the pockets of his countrymen', although Insull, like Fisk, did give his city an opera house.) Some idea of the collapse of Chicago is given in an account by Edmund Wilson in his *American Earthquake*:

> Those who want to keep clear of the jail-like shelters get along as they can in the streets and huddle at night under the Loop or build shacks on empty lots. On whatever waste-places they are permitted to live, the scabby-looking barnacles appear, knocked together from old tar paper and tin, old car bodies, old packing boxes, with stovepipes leaning askew, amid the blackened weeds in the snow, and the bones of old rubbish piles . . . The inhabitants of these wretched settlements chiefly forage from the city dumps, as do many of those whom charity will not help or who, for one reason or another will not go to it or for whom the relief they get is inadequate. There is not a garbage dump in Chicago which is not diligently haunted by the hungry. Last summer in the hot weather when the smell was sickening and the flies were thick there were a hundred people a day coming to one of the dumps, falling on the heap of refuse as soon as the truck had pulled out and digging in it with stick and hands . . . A private incinerator at Thirty-fifth and La Salle Streets which disposes

of the garbage from restaurants and hotels, has been regularly visited by people, in groups of as many as twenty at a time, who pounce on anything that looks edible before it is thrown into the furnace.

The Outfit ate in the restaurants on La Salle, as did the ostensibly respectable 'malefactors of great wealth', in Roosevelt's phrase: the hungry scratched for their leavings. The Outfit set up soup kitchens in the city. President Hoover, who was thought to dislike Capone for a particular reason – the press had rushed to the gangster rather than the president when they were at the same Miami hotel – was under the usual Republican pressure not to help the poor and unemployed since it might encourage them in their idleness. Murray Humphreys did not despair. He evolved a scheme which was to reverberate down the years (see Chapter 12). With hindsight one can recognise, as with all his schemes, how obvious it was, the solution to his difficulties, yet no one else at the time had his vision. If it was the case that Mayor Cermak was in cahoots with Roger Tuohy then something had to be done. On the other hand, Humphreys could not be sure of this – indeed as I suggest in Chapter 13, had he been sure his conduct would have been more drastic. What he did was to frame Tuohy on a kidnap charge, the victim being a fraudster by the name of Factor. Since it was universally known that Humphreys was the master of kidnapping, there was a feeling that Tuohy had been set up. The second part of the plan was to murder Cermak, which was accomplished in Miami to excited dismay. Here was a reforming mayor of Chicago gunned down at the side of his friend President Roosevelt: the nation mourned. The nation, unlike Humphreys, did not know that Cermak promised to raise gangsterism to the level of government. Not that Humphreys' concern was for the public weal, rather it was to restore a more equitable distribution of the spoils between Chicago's City Hall and Cook County, and the Outfit or Syndicate he was temporarily heading. Frank the Enforcer Nitti was probably the assassin.

Cermak had recognised that the election of Roosevelt would lead to the repeal of the Volstead Act and the end of

Prohibition. His plans were laid to rule the about-to-be-respectable speakeasies along with the gambling rackets. His mentors, Hinky Dink and the Bath, had been respectfully laid to rest. Humphreys had Cermak's understanding – and equally mourned the dynamic duo – and had opened negotiations already with major operators such as Joe Kennedy, the future president's father. The Camel's industrial experience had taught him another lesson: there was a lot of money to be made in respectable business, especially when the power of the gun lay behind commercial decisions. 'Why,' as Bertolt Brecht had it, 'rob a bank when you could own one?'

To kill Mayor Cermak and cause Roger Tuohy to be in jail were not, in themselves, more than gestures in the crisis Humphreys saw facing the Outfit. The murder of Capone's soldiers had ended and for this the troops were grateful to Humphreys or, as he saw they saw it, Nitti. Nevertheless Capone and Guzik were going to jail for a long time for not paying income tax. (Guzik, the accountant, was not long gone; Capone was never to return. Not even the ingenuity of Humphreys could find a way to release Little Caesar from the new prison of Alcatraz off the Californian coast. He had not yet mastered federal politics.) The suggestion is that ever since the Pineapple Primary Humphreys had found public displays of violence both unpleasant and counter-productive, that he had disapproved of Capone's crazy murderous exhibitions in elections. This piety strikes the historian many years later as odd given that Humphreys originally established his pre-eminence in the business and trade union world by dreadful thuggery and intimidation with acid and guns. People who knew him say he saw no contradiction but rather took a Chicagoan view that politics was one thing, business was another. This may also have been part of his Welsh inheritance.

He re-established relations with the Democratic party and met the members of the new machine at City Hall led by the Kelly-Nash group. Mayor Kelly was advancing the Cermak policy of running the gambling and saloon business. Tom Nash, a lawyer who defended gangsters, was briefly Cook County Treasurer. Humphreys came to an arrangement with them, but gave his mind more to the manner in which the Outfit or Syndicate should move forward. He bought a large Stars and Stripes flag and placed it behind the front door of his new house on South Bennet Street. About now – 1933 – he also bought a first edition of the songs of the Irish poet Thomas Moore, whose verses he liked to sing, and some valuable early Dickens.

On 27 June 1933 Humphreys was indicted for defrauding the government by not paying tax from 1930 to 1932. The Cook County grand jury had also indicted him and Capone for their kidnapping, bombings and killings in the laundry and linen business. Since Capone was anyway in jail, Humphreys was the principal defendant. As the indictment put it: 'Public Enemy No.1, heir to Scarface Al Capone's power, the brains of the so-called Syndicate and the directing agent behind the muscle-men and killers who have dominated numerous unions and so-called trade associations.' The Camel did not stay in the United States to answer these charges, but took a trip south of the Border, into Mexico.

The Camel stayed in Mexico for sixteen months enjoying himself with his recently married wife, fishing, shooting and evolving a new strategy for himself and the post-Capone epoch. In 1934 he eventually returned to face the courts and, brushing aside more serious charges, was arraigned for not paying income tax on a ransom he had received for one of his kidnapping enterprises. Since he had never been arrested or charged for the kidnapping he, like others, thought it amusing that he was expected to pay income tax on a transaction which had never officially occurred. In court he gallantly asserted that he alone was responsible for whatever it was he had not done, which led to the release of others – and increased therefore the admiration for him among the criminal classes: here was a real 'stand-up guy'. The Camel went off to Leavenworth prison. 'While I'm down there, I intend to study English and maybe a little geometry.' While he was there his wife Mary wrote the prison governor a letter in a prose style so elegant that had there not been the charm of the man himself, his prompt release would not have been unexpected. There is a view that his was a tactical withdrawal, a piece of behaviour rather in the style of the

Duke of Wellington whom he admired. Indeed contrasting his approach with Capone's he might have been taken with an analogy: Wellington maintained that 'Napoleon was looking to fight battles, I was looking to avoid them.'

Humphreys certainly had not liked being represented – in the charge against him in court – as 'Public Enemy No. 1, heir to Scarface Al Capone's power'. When he returned to Chicago from prison his peers recognised his eminence but he had succeeded in making others the object of publicity. He did not want the limelight. This may be because he had learned that those in the light are shot down. In the dark, there is a long life. Or it may simply be that he was so complicated a man that he found it more interesting, more amusing, more mischievous to sit and brood and guide and fructify the Outfit so that it reached into society. Luck was to attend him on his release. If his plan to move the Outfit's money into major United States corporations was already clear, his schemes whereby he was able to bring it about were smiled on. No one will ever know where the laundered money went. It is possible to detect, though, where the Camel, by cajolery, bribery and intellectual daring, created new oases. Quietly he asserted the virtue of his analysis and, from time to time, would offer a bravura display for the benefit of his admirers and the increasing dismay of such authorities as were not in his pocket.

9 The Double Jeopardy triumph

When any member of organised crime became involved in
any kind of trial, then it was the duty of Humphreys to
mastermind the defence, the strategy involved in defending that particular associate of his.
William Roemer, FBI agent, in conversation, 1983

McLane's action, at the opening of the trial, brought a
smile of understanding from Murray Humphreys, one of
the seven defendants, who, like Nitti, was one of the chiefs
of the old Capone gang. He beamed upon the man the
State had expected to crush the gangsters, put on his coat,
and departed from the courtroom before most of the
crowd comprehended the significance of McLane's move.
Chicago Tribune, 30 November 1940

In the scholarly debates which still continue in FBI circles
about which of all Humphreys' legal manoeuvres was the
most brilliant, one school of thought maintains it was his
novel use of the Fifth Amendment in court and Senate hearings. At his Oklahoma home his own fretwork carving of the
sentence 'I refuse to answer on the grounds that I might
incriminate myself' – and its prominent place among
mementoes shows that he himself was proud of establishing such a precedent in American criminology. Another
school holds, however, that his general conduct of the
defence (nominally, the faithful congressman Libonati was
the defence attorney) in the Bartenders' Union trial in
Chicago in 1940 represents a higher achievement. After all,
he himself, for the only time in his life, was on trial on a

serious charge. The State had never been so confident of success, the celebrations were prepared, the newspapers alerted for, at last, the defeat of the Outfit, the triumph of the forces of the law.

The case, placed in the perspective of the city's chronicle of mayhem, was not especially lurid. George B. McLane who for twenty-eight years had been the business agent of the Bartenders' Union in Chicago, accused a Louis Romano and the Outfit or Syndicate of interfering in the affairs of the union, stealing its funds and attempting to displace him. He was joined in his action by two other officials, his brother Michael and William Salvatore. There were 4400 members in his local or union branch, paying $220,000 a year in dues. George McLane was asking for an injunction to restrain the gangsters who would otherwise, among other serious matters, at once walk away with $125,000 from a fund designed as benefits for members. In support of this claim McLane's lawyer A. C. Lewis produced a thirty-two-page brief which set out the history of the union and the part the mob had played in its affairs. On the strength of it the State moved not only against the corrupt union leaders but against Frank the Enforcer Nitti and Murray Humphreys. It might not be a murder charge against two men who had strolled away from so many, who had commanded so many more but surely, now, they would go to jail. The charge was 'conspiracy to injure a man in his employment', one punishable by 'a one- to five-year sentence in prison as the maximum'.

Chicagoans were aware of the importance of the trial. It was rich in cultural associations. The Bartenders' Union was one supposedly respectable inheritance of Prohibition, its members the rank and file of the legal sale of booze. There was, though, a general suspicion that waiters and waitresses, along with bartenders, were being run by thugs. Joey Aiuppa, who had procured machine guns for Dillinger and other murderers, was thought to be involved. (Aiuppa was later to irritate Humphreys by forgetting the few words involved in pleading the Fifth Amendment before the Senate in Washington, and then finding it difficult to read them when Humphreys had had them typed.) There were souls, more optimistic than history had taught them to be, who saw in the trial a vicious circle's conclusion, who, believing that such crime as they had seen, having begun in speak-easies, would so end with the bootleggers' jailing. McLane's attorney, A. C. Lewis, certainly took a grand view of the occasion and of his fortune to have in his sights both Capone's successor as Public Enemy Number One and the Camel's nominated inheritor Nitti. He should have known better, but Humphreys' legal gifts were not then generally known. Attorney Lewis offered the court an account running into tens of thousands of words of the union's origins and the Outfit's intrusions, much of it familiar, some of its 1940 rhetoric striking: 'The Chicago Syndicate was the originator of the now famous Hitler policy of disposing separately of each person who interfered with its designs.'

What Attorney Lewis wished to prove was that Louis Romano, who had become president of the union, and his associates James Crowley and Tom Panton, were members of the mob; and that they had been imposed on the union by Humphreys, Nitti and a mysterious character named Frederick Evans. (Evans, a well-known and well-thought-of accountant, was to be murdered in the late fifties by friends of Roger Tuohy who, it was believed, had lately been killed on the instructions of Humphreys: the slogan 'don't get mad, get even', had unusual force in the Camel's conduct always, but sometimes in that of his enemies too.) Of Frank Nitti, Attorney Lewis observed that

> he was high in the councils of the Capone gang and was generally reputed to be the person who carried out the executions decreed by the gang and became known as Nitti the Enforcer. In the course of time Al Capone was sent to prison on an income tax charge. His gang was so well established that it continued to function, and continued to take on new activities. It became known as the Syndicate and the aforesaid Frank Nitti became the titular head thereof.

The lawyer then went on to describe, in language poignant in the circumstances, both the aspirations of the union and the fate that fell on it:

85

Labour unions are usually organised as voluntary unin-
corporated associations. They are intended to be very
democratic in the management of their affairs. Their
primary purpose is to better working conditions and establish equitable and satisfactory wage scales for the members,
and for that purpose it is their effort to organise completely
the industry to which the particular union might appertain.
The activities of the union require permanent officers and
the establishment and maintenance of permanent offices . . .
In many instances to protect familes of members of
the union who die they have established a death-benefit
fund . . . In many instances said unions have prudently
accumulated a large sum of money.

Having established the existence of these funds, Attorney
Lewis then offers an account of how the Outfit operated, a
narrative as true for all the other unions in which Humphreys
interested himself as for the bartenders of Chicago:

The unions have become a battlefield for gang activities.
They have developed a technique known by the slang expression of 'muscling-in'. The emissaries of the Syndicate
by threats of violence and death, forced the unions to
pay them large sums of money. In many instances they
forced their own agents into the offices of the union, took
charge of their treasury and of their business. They packed
meetings with men under their control, and so terrorised
the general membership of the union as to prevent the
members from attending meetings. Their reputations as
criminals and murderers were such that union officials and
members were afraid to resist their demands.

At which the lawyer points the finger on behalf of clients
McLane and Salvatore at Humphreys and Nitti:

In the year 1934 and in the early part of 1935 the
Bartenders' Union through George McLane was attempting to organise the men working in the bars and taverns
in Chicago. Among them were bartenders working in
taverns owned by the Syndicate, although there was no

way of knowing which bars and taverns were owned by the old Capone mob. The Union had pickets. Our pickets and business agents, including George McLane, were threatened. Many were slugged. On one Saturday in the early part of March 1935 McLane received a telephone call from some person who represented himself as an emissary of the Syndicate, demanding a sum of $500. McLane refused to accede to the demand at which the emissary called and described what would happen to him if he refused to pay. Being coerced McLane then hired Louis Romano as a Union agent. The slugging of pickets immediately ceased. The members of the picketed bars joined the union . . . Humphreys, Evans and Romano then moved into the office and told McLane that the war was on and he would be the first casualty. Humphreys then told McLane that he would be much safer if he took a long vacation outside the State of Illinois. McLane, knowing the reputation of Humphreys, did leave the State for three months. His authority to countersign cheques was revoked and Louis Romano took over the function. By January 1940 Romano had called a meeting of all Union agents to tell them that he was the boss and that he was going to show them what muscle meant. McLane was put out of his office. The Union was controlled by the Syndicate.

The next step for Attorney Lewis was to present this powerful case in court and win an injunction for his clients McLane and Salvatore. To their delight and that of the State and the government in Washington, he won. The union structure was to be dissolved. The Syndicate stooge Romano was to be fired; there were to be honest union elections; Humphreys and Nitti were indicted on the strength of this triumph for the forces of good: the next trial, in November, would see the back of the agents of murder and corruption. If, in City Hall, or in more elevated palaces of government, there were sceptics puzzled that the elusive Humphreys had been so simply netted, who tried to detect a mystery, then they were silent. Joy was, publicly, universal: come November, so was bewilderment.

The great strategist, the puppet-master, always has the

advantage over his opponents, as Humphreys was to demonstrate in this case. He knows the objective, they do not. The writer of fiction similarly has the edge: but here the Camel was not manipulating figures of his imagination but powerful elements in Chicago society and the United States. With hindsight we can see that the State of Illinois should not have been quite so shocked by the Camel's November *coup*. He had shown his hand earlier in the month in a different case in a different Chicago court. But since no one could see his cards, indeed not even guess at what game he was playing, prosecutor, judge or police can scarcely be blamed. Trying to piece his gambit together even now is not easy, its boldness fresh after nearly half a century.

The scene is this. In the Criminal Court in Chicago a jury is, day by day, being selected and sworn in for the major trial of Nitti and Humphreys. The public is bribing court officials to win seats for the drama. Meanwhile in the same building but in a lesser court an odd manoeuvre is being conducted in a minor, seemingly routine affair which seems to have no direct connection with the big trial – except, of course, that it was, in Humphreys' mind, very, very, directly connected.

George McLane, the witness who was to send Humphreys to jail, was appearing in the case in the lesser court. His attorney, Lewis, was there. The honest Mr Lewis, persuaded that within days his client McLane was going to appear against Humphreys and Nitti and break the Outfit, was innocently offering a new argument on behalf of McLane's trade union. Whereas previously he had argued successfully for putting the Bartenders' Union into receivership so that it could make a pristine new start, he was now saying that there was no need for this receivership. His client McLane was now happy that the union was healthy. The crooked Louis Romano was no longer a nuisance. And, of course, Humphreys and Nitti were soon to go to jail. No longer would the gangsters be a threat. Attorney Lewis – and who could blame him – was taken in by all this. He was a shade bewildered when Louis Romano suddenly appeared with a lawyer wishing to join in the general parade of sweetness and light. This might have suggested that perhaps there was something odd going on, but Attorney Lewis, like any reasonable lawyer, thought that he had carried out his client's instructions. George B. McLane, the good guy, had regained control of his union, was free of the dreadful Nitti and Humphreys and was now about to appear at the Criminal Court as the key witness to help the State send the Camel to jail.

Came the opening of the big trial, the State poised, the public agog. Attorney Lewis was met at the court with the news that he was no longer representing his client George McLane. There was no time for an explanation, and, had there been one possible, it's unlikely anyone would have had the face to utter it. The vital witness would instead be represented by a former judge, Alfar Eberhardt. This lawyer was known, by those who knew such things in Chicago, to be one of Murray Humphreys' old pals, one of those judges he would place in particular courts when the needs of the Outfit demanded sympathy. Had there been time for close analysis, the observer would have sensed that peculiar developments lay ahead. Here was McLane with his union back in his hands, having sworn that he was no longer in fear of Humphreys, arriving for the major drama without his honest lawyer but instead with one of the Camel's stooges. The Welshman strolled into the Criminal Court with his lawyer Congressman Libonati in tow, smiling courteously at the assembly, placing his vicuna coat on the back of his chair and 'gracing' the judge with a nod.

State Prosecutor William B. Crawford opened his case in a courtroom as crowded as the city had seen for a while – and why not, when before them they had two of Capone's inheritors, presented together for their come-uppance? Mr Crawford explained that one of his witnesses, William Salvatore, had been missing for a few months but that he expected him to appear that day to support the evidence that his union leader George McLane was so vitally going to offer. Prosecutor Crawford then began the recital of the testimony which McLane had offered in another court and which he was about to repeat and so dish the Syndicate. Humphreys, Nitti and the four acolyte hoods charged with them listened to this speech by the excited prosecutor with, contemporary accounts have it, 'polite interest'. George McLane was called. The *Chicago Tribune* reported:

In response to a question by Crawford he stated his name and gave his age as 50 years and his residence as 2911 Lunt Avenue. It was the next question which brought the bombshell.

'What is your wife's given name?'

'I must refuse to answer,' said McLane in a voice so low it was scarcely audible, 'on the ground that it might tend to incriminate me.'

Q. 'You know the defendant Murray Humphreys?'

A. 'I must refuse to answer on the grounds that it might incriminate me.'

Crawford asked the same question regarding each of the other defendants. McLane chanted the same answer to each question.

Q. 'Why do you refuse to answer?'

A. 'On the advice of my attorney.'

Q. 'Who is your attorney?'

A. 'Former Judge Alfar Eberhardt.'

Throughout which colloquy, as the *Tribune* reported, Murray Humphreys had been beaming at the witness; and was the first to put on his coat and leave the Criminal Court, as prosecutors, judge, police and public sat agape. The trial was over.

The first man publicly to respond to the drama was the bewildered Attorney Lewis:

I am sure the hand of Nitti [not, note, Humphreys] reached into the Courtroom and palsied McLane with terror. There is no other explanation for his action. It may be that he still can be induced to tell the truth to the Criminal Court jury – I don't know. I want it understood that I am not a party to McLane's present conduct. When I told Judge Dunne last week that I believed Nitti had burned his fingers in grabbing the Bartenders' Union and had let go and would never again molest the union members, I made that statement in good faith. Now I am not so sure about it. I started in this lawsuit as a crusader. I expected to get results that would benefit trade unionism and the public generally. I believe we were making headway. If McLane had gone through with the prosecution of Nitti his action would have had a great influence in cleaning up rotten union affairs in this city.

Which is precisely why Murray Humphreys could not allow McLane to go through with the prosecution. For Humphreys the McLane affair was far more significant than the commonplace exercise of muscle. On the simplest level, if in a fashion unusual even in Chicago, he had demonstrated to the authorities in the city and in Washington – and, more importantly, to the Syndicate and friends in New York and Los Angeles – that he possessed a strategic grasp of defence. Thus he had chosen not to intimidate McLane before the trial had opened, which was the vulgar, murderous tactic of the twenties and thirties. On the contrary, he had encouraged the holding of the trial. Therefore, when the trial collapsed as soon as it opened, but after arraignment and indictment, then those charged could never be charged again for their alleged offence. The rule of Double Jeopardy protected them: a citizen cannot have his freedom, his innocence, put so in jeopardy twice on the same charge.

Since it is improbable that the Camel went through this charade just for the fun of it – although some of his friends believe him capable of so doing – what was his objective? One colleague does hold that he wanted to try, one day, every legal gambit he had learned from Judge Murray, just as a chess player will essay an esoteric grand master's ploy, or a pianist, Bach-arranged-by-Busoni; and it wasn't long, after all, since the judge had died, and Humphreys always felt a debt. And that same colleague in the Outfit suggests, more, that Humphreys set up the whole thing, even persuading McLane in the very beginning to employ Attorney Lewis to work up a case against Nitti, himself and others. So, while that reading is improbable, certainly it is the case that the consequences of the whole affair were of benefit to the Welsh-American gangster. So many lessons were carried to so many, even if it was decades before some were discovered.

The McLane Affair was Humphreys' way of showing that the propaganda of the deed did not have to be the machine gun and the pineapple, as in the Capone days: the new style could be witnessed in open court.

When the authorities had recovered from the shock of McLane's dreadful defection and Humphreys' affable departure – and had grasped that he had told them, in effect, not to pursue the Outfit through other unions or businesses in Chicago since, who knows, the law, not Humphreys, might again have a come-uppance – it took them some time to grasp that these men were best pursued in other cities. The Camel was ahead of them even in this analysis. Indeed it was yet another strand in his conduct of the defence that November in 1940 to demonstrate to his colleagues that he was quite in control of a far more serious game than the one they had been tormenting the bartenders of Chicago with throughout the thirties. Along with Frank the Enforcer Nitti and two other of his co-defendants that day – Louis Little New York Campagna and Paul Ricca – Humphreys was well on the way to taking over the Hollywood movie industry. His performance in the Chicago courtroom reassured them. The Camel's repute as a stand-up guy since he had done time at Leavenworth was solid. Now he had shown that he could take the Outfit into court and mock, and win, with style. How were they to grasp that the fun their colleague derived from living on 'the dangerous edge of things' was not always going to be their fun; that within four years they would be indicted and, two of them, jailed over the Hollywood scandal, while Humphreys was not even questioned. The third, Frank Nitti, was to kill himself when arrested in the next remarkable case.

The birthplace at Carno in mid-Wales of Murray Humphreys' father. A depression in agriculture towards the end of the nineteenth century led many Welsh to migrate. The small farmhouse was named Y Castell (the Castle) because it commanded the valley. The name seems to have encouraged patrician traits in the family.

Left: Murray's parents, Welsh-speaking Brian and Ann. The mother was a clever dignified woman, the father given to using his son's money to gamble. Brian Humphreys' brother became a Justice of the Peace in Wales. The parents appear, as here, in many of Murray Humphreys' home movies.

Below right: Humphreys, the youngest child, remained fond of his brother and sisters, so much so that he placed his older brother, Ernest, in the cinema business to facilitate its corruption.

The beautiful child Llewelyn Morris Humphreys, as he was originally called, contemplates the beginning of the twentieth century in Chicago.

At the age of sixteen Humphreys re-christened himself 'Murray' in honour of a judge who had befriended him, impressed by the young newspaper seller's spirit and intelligence. Many young Chicagoans, like Humphreys, could supplement their income by fraudulent voting for the Democratic machine run by 'Hinky Dink', an alderman. He paid three dollars a vote. There was also burglary, for which Murray Humphreys was arrested in 1916.

Humphreys' wife Mary Brendle was half Irish and half Cherokee. Her mother had survived the 'trail of tears' when the United States government marched the Cherokee into the wastes of Oklahoma. Her business acumen led to her being the only woman privy to the Outfit's finances.

Humphreys' elegance was celebrated and became more marked in the late Twenties when he became Al Capone's agent in corrupting laundry management and trade unions. His jokes about 'laundering' money, about people being taken to the cleaners, were thought to be original. 'Vote early and vote often' was his advice to Chicago's electorate.

The St Valentine Day Massacre of 1929 remains the most notorious of the Outfit's m
that Capone was intent on killing a rival, Bugs Moran, out of rage at a double-cross i
arrived late. The man who most benefited from the massacre was Murray Humphrey
was his only serious rival in the laundry 'rackets'. The murders took place only a few
birthplace.

Below left: The fact of being crooked always sparked his wit. When he built his daugl
so designed it that it, too, was crooked. This plaque hangs in his Oklahoma house.

Below right: According to the FBI Humphreys was the first person to advise mobsters
Amendment. This and other legal stratagems account for much of the awe and fury h
Attorney-General Robert Kennedy. This plaque, also hanging in his Oklahoma house

Humphreys attracted an unusual number of nicknames. In public he was known mostly as the 'Camel' or 'Murray the Hump', the latter from his surname, the former deriving from the latter. His friends usually knew him as 'Curly' from his fine head of hair. 'Moneybags', the 'Clever Hood', 'Einstein of the Mob' were other journalistic terms.

eceived opinion is
ze war. But Moran
e of those killed
m Humphreys'

ll garden house he

the Fifth
d, especially from
wife's favourite.

VER
MIGHT
ME

One of Humphreys' handguns which the author held in his hand. There are three notches in the butt. There is no record of how many murders Humphreys committed in the gang wars since he was never charged with any.

When Murray Humphreys asked his daughter Llewella whom she would like to come and entertain at her Graduation from High School, she asked for the young Frank Sinatra. He came. Most other of the great American entertainers would have been just as happy to oblige.

Humphreys seldom appeared in his own films since he did not regard them as frivolous home movies, but as properly crafted works. He would draw titles for them and give thought to the soundtrack. Filming the island of Alcatraz, where many of his colleagues, including Capone, were incarcerated, he used the tune The Gang's All Here.

Humphreys' final public appearance — the day before his death in 1965 — was to sign a bond granting him bail. He turned to the TV reporter, Jorie Lueloff, who asked him for his comments on the new predicament he found himself in. His answer — that he thought her a very pretty girl — delighted his audience.

Murray Humphreys' daughter Llewella (or Luella) became a concert pianist because her father had said he would like her to be one. She gave three concerts with the Rome Symphony Orchestra and then retired. She was married, for a while, to the Italian actor Rossano Brazzi. Today she lives mostly in Oklahoma.

In his fifties Humphreys was persuaded to answer a subpoena demanding his presence before a Federal Grand Jury in Chicago to discover what he knew about organised crime in the United States. He astonished the court by appearing as a lame, shabby, half-blind inarticulate. He was excused, left the court and once outside, threw away stick and eye-patch and skipped through the bars of Rush Street buying drinks for cronies. He seldom drank himself.

10   Look out, Hollywood, here I come

The Outfit, through the unions, controlled every facet of the movie industry. And it all started with my mother: she was a fan, crazy about movie stars. So she mentioned to my father, why don't we go into this business so that I can meet everybody. So he, eventually, could make or break a studio by calling people out on strike. He loved making his own films, too, editing, doing the titles and putting on the sound-tracks when sound came in. On holidays it was a nuisance with mother and myself twiddling our thumbs while he set up the camera.
Llewella Humphreys, in conversation, 1983

When Nitti, Ricca, Campagna, Pearce and the others were indicted in 1943 in the Hollywood trial, the word came down that Humphreys would be charged because everyone knew he was there. But somehow it never happened.
Art Petaque, *Chicago Sun-Times*, in conversation, 1983

Humphreys was involved in that case as much as any of the people who went to jail but the prosecution witnesses, Bioff and Browne, wouldn't give evidence against him because of their affection and regard for Humphreys.
William Roemer, FBI agent, in conversation, 1983

Since Humphreys alone in the courtroom had known that he would have the rest of the day free, his first celebration of his Double Jeopardy success was to walk down Madison to the Loop and buy ten rolls of 16-mm colour film. He had in mind a surprise Christmas present for his family. Throughout the thirties he had been shooting brief, black-and-white 8-mm films of parents, wife and daughter, fellow hoods. He was now going to try to make a long colour film because he planned to make many more on a journey to Hawaii, Hollywood and San Francisco.

He made the Christmas film and he made the travel films and, more than forty years later when his daughter Llewella showed them to me, I was astonished, so much so that it is difficult to unravel the skeins of surprise. First, here was the man himself, elegant and handsome as described, looking very like his friend, the actor Fred MacMurray. Here was his voice, harder perhaps than his admirers had suggested. Here were the jokes one had heard were characteristic. In one film, as the ship on which he is returning from Pearl Harbor to San Francisco passes Alcatraz island where his friend Al Capone had been imprisoned and gone mad, Humphreys chooses to place on the film's sound-track the tune, 'The Gang's All Here'. In the sequences describing life in the Pacific islands Humphreys the narrator offers an earnest didacticism to become common decades later in television documentaries about life on earth in general. We learn how coffee is made. There is a dissertation on the growing of pineapples in which, reasonably enough, a giggle is just suppressed.

The domestic film is charming. We see Mrs Humphreys prepare the Christmas tree, lamps alight, the presents cornucopial. The cinéaste himself is seen tucking his seven-year-old daughter into bed. She reflects. She jumps out of bed and, father watching, kneels to say her prayers. And then it is the morning of Christmas and the young Llewella opens her scores of presents, holds before her a silk dress. The delights of the day continue to be paraded. The family arrive: Grandpa and Grandma – in Welsh, *Taid, Nain* – the brother and sister of the host, nieces and nephews; a black servant brings in the turkey. The portrait of this happy, even perfect American family (given that they are so evidently prosperous when the Depression is not yet over) is enhanced by a brief sequence showing the head of the household at the door wearing a long vicuna coat, kissing everyone farewell alongside a large Stars and Stripes.

Humphreys' films are made with skill, enthusiasm and affection. And while it is the case that no one who has ever been involved with any kind of film-making would suppose that a moral sense is a qualification for the trade – indeed, the converse could be more likely – the time and craft offered to his hobby by the great hood do substantiate his daughter's bewilderment about him. How could she square this manifestly witty and kind man with his murderous repute in the public prints? And those jolly Italians in father's more primitive black-and-white flicks, at the swimming pool in Florida, at the race-track, fishing off their colony – Cuba, the Outfit's playground – so familial, so domesticated: could they be murderers, too? They could and some of them, although hard to recognise in the 8-mm home movies, were to be involved in one of the cinéaste's masterpieces.

It is very unlikely that the Camel needed much encouragement from his star-struck wife to give his mind, even at a very busy period in his life, to the matter of Hollywood. Chicago citizens were peculiarly aware of the cinema. The city's chauvinist newspapers reminded them that in the early days of the movies, one-fifth of all the films in the world were made in Chicago. Hadn't Wallace Beery, Lewis Stone, Tom Mix, Gloria Swanson and Edward Arnold begun their careers there? Hadn't the moguls Carl Laemmle and Adolph Zukor opened studios on the North Side before they set out for California? One version of the cause of the migration is that the country west of Chicago was being so developed that it was hard to find territory for Westerns any more in 1910 and, moreover, the weather was terrible. Another is that the Patents Company was harassing the film-makers and, worse, that the Chicago theatre proprietors were stealing prints and making life difficult. It was easier to hide in California. True, President Wilson when he, a sympathetic Democrat, came to the White House, revoked the Patent Trust laws in 1913 and helped the Laemmles and Zukors. By then, the Hollywood climate had come to seem more suitable for filming.

Given that the cinema had a particular historical appeal for Chicagoans in general, for Capone's friends and inheritors the attraction was mesmerising. To own the night clubs where the famous jazzmen played, where celebrities sang, to command the restaurants and brothels, to shoot people in the foyer in the Opera House, to have judges and politicians and cops dancing to their tune: that was life. But then to stroll through the Loop with heavily armed bodyguards and walk into a movie theatre and see yourself on the screen: who in history had enjoyed such fame? Unfortunately, none of the gangsters seems to have been articulate or reflective enough to have recorded any considered aesthetic appraisal of the experience of seeing their lives depicted in movies that were to entrance the world. What would Richard III or Henry IV think of Shakespeare? That the mob enjoyed *Scarface*, *Public Enemy Number One* and the hundreds of major or B movies that were to represent their contribution to Chicago and American culture is clear both from their attendances at the showings and their refusal to influence films in the making, when they easily might have. There is no sign that they were angry that the notorious former Chicago reporter Ben Hecht had begun the Hollywood stampede into gangster films with *Scarface*. The Outfit's response to the cinematic new wave was practical, at first, fitful, even incoherent: there was something, or someone, missing.

Al Capone and his immediate colleagues were preoccupied late in 1929 with the fuss about the St Valentine Day Massacre and did not pay much notice to Tommy Maloy when he called on them. Maloy was having some trouble in his union, the International Association of Theatrical Stage Employees (IATSE). His members were the stagehands in the making of movies but, more relevantly, at least to the day's business, also operated the projectors in the movie houses. The structure of the IATSE union was such that membership was restricted, so that some operators were required to pay for a 'permit' to work. These latter thought this procedure a racket, and were restive. Mr Maloy would like them persuaded of the virtue of the system.

Two very junior members of the Outfit were loaned to Tommy Maloy. One was Willie Bioff who, by Bob Thomas' account in *King Cohn*, his biography of the Hollywood producer Harry Cohn, 'had the figure of a Greek wrestler and the morals of a panderer, which he once was'. The other was George Browne, 'a likeable jughead and Good-time Charlie around the Loop', as the *Daily News* succinctly had it. Bioff and Browne did not need the sharpest of minds to recognise, once they had solved Mr Maloy's immediate difficulty by threatening a few workers, that they had arrived in a profitable office. They decided to stay, so much so that after four years Tommy Maloy became convinced that if he couldn't find help, then he would lose his union to the mob, a way so many seemed to be going those days. He made a decision which even in the scarcely credible annals of Chicago must rank as the most crazy. Indeed it is hard to think of any other single piece of folly with quite such consequences not only for poor Tommy Maloy, but for his workers, for the entertainment world in the United States thereafter, and for the repute of some of the nation's most distinguished political leaders. He had heard that Murray Humphreys was just out of Leavenworth prison. He turned to 'the brainy hood' to seek salvation.

It may be that Maloy had heard the word around the Windy City. The Camel had not cared for the title awarded him of Public Enemy Number One, the buzz went, not merely because of his sensitive nature, his fastidiousness, but because it was unfair. More, that he had chosen to go to jail to remove himself from his past and its dreadful repute. And so Maloy took his concerns to this man expert in the ways of the Syndicate, the poacher, as he thought, turned game-keeper or, if not quite that, at least a heavy neutral. Murray Humphreys was pleased to meet him. He too had considered the prospects of Maloy's IATSE union. More, his wife had suggested that it would be nice to take over Hollywood, to extend the Chicago business to California perhaps. He agreed to help. Within three months Tommy Maloy was dead. As the *Daily News* put it many years later:

In February 1935, shortly after this last desperate bid to recover control of his union by asking Humphreys to get the Capone guys off his neck, Maloy was blown out of his automobile on the Outer Drive near Soldier Field by a blast of shotguns held by 'dark-complectioned' men and he, like so many who had approached the flame, was carried away to another inquest at which the assassins were identified as 'person or persons unknown'.

97

Even before Tommy Maloy's murder, though, the plan was in place. The annual meeting of the union at Louisville, Kentucky, had elected George Browne as its President, any members reluctant to support him probably being impressed by the presence in the town of gangsters from most parts of America. There was Lucky Luciano, Meyer Lansky, Benjamin 'Bugsy' Siegel. Less celebrated then was John Rosseli, a Humphreys' protégé, who was to benefit for a while, but to meet his Maker wrapped in concrete in the Florida Keys; how, though, it must have looked to Rosseli at the time – to be about to marry film actress June Lang, to be rich, to mix with the famous, to achieve the American dream: such wonders could the Camel work for his friends.

The election over, Willie Bioff was sent briskly to California. The new union president Browne was drinking so much by this time that nobody, including himself, knew where he was most days. Humphreys was unhappy with the state of the union in Hollywood. There had been a strike of the craft unions in 1933 which the workers had lost badly. The bargaining position was weak: the employers were too strong. A less resolute figure would have hesitated. Mass unemployment had become endemic, it seemed, in the United States. To have a job at all was good fortune. Even if President Roosevelt had just come to power with promises of a New Deal, scepticism was abroad. The cinema industry, too, had become a means of softening the anguish of the people. Exactly: the troubled nation needed the dream factory, did it not? The analysis made: action.

Before setting Willie Bioff to work in Hollywood, Humphreys placed his own brother Ernest in the business in Chicago as a cinema operator. (The city legend is that Ernest never worked even one shift, but that when government agents searching for the Camel might go to the cinema where Ernest was supposed to be, looking for guidance, they would never find the brother but always several hoods in the audience watching gangster films, all on the same quest.) The tactics to be followed at Paramount, Fox, Warners' or whichever, were familiar. First control the union, then use that power to shake down the owners. In a little over a year the demoralised union was rebuilt and much, much more.

Where in 1934 there were fewer than two hundred union members, by 1936 there was one union only and it had twelve thousand members. Those who might have wanted to see their small craft unions revived were knocked on the head. The promise from Bioff was that if everyone joined him they would have the power to stop production. Where else were Louis B. Mayer, Sam Goldwyn and Harry Warner going to find labour to make their so-profitable films? And just you watch: we'll have a closed shop, too. And they did.

The ground secured, it was now time for the advance. Bioff was instructed by Humphreys to approach the studio owners. Would they care to make a handsome contribution? Or would they prefer a strike? Very expensive, strikes. By 1937 Nicholas Schenck was paying $200,000 on behalf of Loew's: after all, it would be a shame if films were made in Hollywood and no cinemas in the United States were able to show them because IATSE operators were on strike. Fox, Paramount and Warners' were paying $100,000 in order to be allowed to make the movies. Columbia were shaken down for only $25,000. By Bob Thomas' biographical account Harry Cohn alone refused to pay.

These sums from the studio owners were small compared with those the mob were extracting from the union, not only in Hollywood but throughout America. Once Humphreys had Browne and Bioff in place and the membership had so remarkably grown in the film studios, they imposed a 2 per cent levy on all forty-two thousand members. This brought in some $1,500,000 in 1937–8. Most of this cash went to Chicago. And if members did not care to pay this 'special assessment' contribution? In Chicago retribution was possibly less harmful than the form it took in Hollywood: in neither case was there, this time around, simple thuggery. In Chicago the Outfit double-crossed union members in a wage dispute with the circuit owners. In Hollywood it brazenly denounced its recalcitrant union members to the studio bosses as communists or anti-American radicals, ensuring dismissal and setting a precedent which was to have such serious consequences in the late forties and early fifties for so many directors and actors.

It was while the gold was flowing so freely that

Humphreys called at this corner of his fiefdom, with family and camera. Dressed to the nines they stroll among exotic plants with the film star Fay Wray (celebrated for her role in *King Kong*) towards a camera operated by hand and eye unremembered. Is it, the colour film proposes, not passing great, as an earlier Marlowe would have put it (not Chandler's), to be a Syndicate king and walk in triumph through Beverly Hills? 'In those days,' Llewella Humphreys told me, 'the studios had no tours, as they have today. Joan Crawford was a very big star, at her peak then. She always worked on a closed set, so that no one could come and see her. Mother really wanted to meet her. But this set that particular day was especially closed because Joan Crawford had a scar on her face in the movie and didn't want anyone to see her. The head of the studio, anyway, took mother and me in. Joan Crawford stopped right in the middle of her scene and said: "Get those two out of here. I will not have it on my set. It's closed." The head of the studio went over to her and told her: "Either they stay or you go, and you are through in pictures." So we watched her make the movie.'

That the vast audiences for Hollywood productions, whether in the United States, Europe or the growing markets elsewhere, had no idea of this close connection between the Chicago mob and the film producers was understandable enough. The law-enforcing officers, however, were equally ignorant. Since the directors, writers and actors certainly knew, their work, with hindsight, has more force than even it seemed to possess at the time. There were many kinds of response to the gangster films, to Edward G. Robinson, James Cagney, Paul Muni and later Humphrey Bogart. To foreigners, at least if my youthful response was characteristic, the films were myth. The street gangster had assumed the equally mythic cowboy role: the sheriff had become the cop or .the often shifty district attorney. With hindsight we can recognise that several film-makers were offering sharp, sometimes savage criticisms of corruption in American life. Ben Hecht and Charles Lederer were to call on their knowledge of Chicago once more in Henry Hathaway's 1947 film *Kiss of Death*. And wasn't there even a film in which Edward G. actually played a Chicago hood who decided to go straight and arrived at Hollywood to be an actor, only to be pursued by his former colleagues in the interests of corruption? *Farewell My Lovely*, based on the Raymond Chandler novel, directed by Edward Dmytryk in 1944, is rich in sinister social atmosphere which now may look more precisely descriptive of Hollywood in Humphreys' heyday than any stranger could have conceived possible at first viewing. Students of the American cinema have noted how many of the most distinguished talents involved in making gangster movies in the forties – Dmytryk, Hammett, Garfield, Adrian Scott – were to be hounded by the Senate Un-American Activities Committee, and were to suffer far more than Murray Humphreys ever did when the US Senate tried to catch him out.

The first step was to prosecute not the gangsters but the leader of the industry Joseph M. Schenck, who was president of the Motion Picture Producers and Distributors of America as well as of the family company Loew's. He went to jail for less than a year but the trial and subsequent investigations revealed that all the major companies had been fiddling their books in the interests of concealing the amount of cash that had been paid to IATSE through Browne and Bioff. The truth was out. Curiously the revelations and the hope that the future might be a more honest one did not win the bosses of Warner Brothers, Paramount and Twentieth Century-Fox the universal shared delight expected. There were sceptics, Bob Thomas reports, 'who wondered whether the payments were aimed merely at forestalling labor trouble in the studios and the theatres. Did the company heads pay Bioff to prevent his rank and file from seeking better contracts? And did they plan to use his union to help destroy minor studios?'

The federal government now had the evidence to indict the union leaders: but in which state, which city? Since the president, George Browne, was usually in his Chicago office, the courtroom there might have seemed the obvious place. There was Los Angeles itself. Common sense, not to mention a wariness hard-won by prosecutors, proposed otherwise if there was to be a chance of winning a conviction which might stick. A discovery had been made which settled the venue. The *Daily News* reported:

In shaking down the great minds of the movie industry, Bioff made his great mistake. Napoleon went to Moscow, after which the dice went against him. Bioff went to New York, which gives New York jurisdiction in the case even though the bundles of currency were carried to Chicago to be cut up between the individual leaders of the mob.

The Camel might always propose: he could not always completely dispose and for reasons little different from those which preoccupied more respectable business management on the sub-continent. 'Personnel' was always to be a problem. Tactics had been excellent in Californiia, income was steady, taxation nil: no one had been shot, even, although many had been leaned on. Unfortunately, not all Humphreys' executives shared his view that life should be lived modestly – that greed, like vulgar display, did not pay either in the short or the long run. So that while Humphreys was content with progress and delighted that he and his wife were making the acquaintance of and, in some celebrated cases, establishing friendships with, stars of screen, stage and radio, the louche Willie Bioff interpreted matters differently. Bioff was taken not so much with the film stars' glamour but rather with the size of their incomes. He decided, without consulting the Camel, to hound the members of the Screen Actors' Guild.

Had the president of the guild in 1940 not been an actor of such intelligence and determination as Robert Montgomery, Bioff might have succeeded. (What if his successor Ronald Reagan had been there?) Montgomery not only warned off Bioff: he borrowed money from the guild's funds to investigate the gangster and to try to substantiate the gossip about extortion in the industry. All information was passed to the *Daily Variety*, whose editor, Arthur Ungar, also did not care for Bioff. Steadily the details appeared of how much the studio heads had paid Bioff and his dipsomaniac union president Browne. The amount of money was so great – millions of dollars – that government in Washington paid serious attention. How should it move?

On 23 May 1941 Bioff and Browne appeared in New York, charged with extortion, and all the heads of the studios in California came east and testified. The union leaders were sentenced to ten years and eight years in jail respectively. Harry Warner, the head of Warner Brothers, made in the course of his evidence a remark which intrigued the prosecution. He testified that in making one $25,000 shakedown during one merry Yule season, Willie Bioff told him that the 'boys in Chicago' wanted a Christmas present. At which District Attorney Correa asked his assistant Boris Kostelanetz (who was brother-in-law of the opera singer Lily Pons) if he would try to discover quite who the 'boys' were since it was improbable that the authorities in Chicago would bend their energies in that direction. Quite why he should have imagined that any sleuth from the rival city of New York would have any luck is not clear. Certainly nothing happened until Willie Bioff, finding the dread prison Alcatraz all he feared, chose freedom and, by informing on his friends in 1943, created a sensation and guaranteed his own murder twelve years later when he was living modestly in Arizona: his car blew up and him with it when he turned the ignition key.

Willie Bioff had reported to district attorneys Correa and Kostelanetz in New York that all the leaders of the Chicago Outfit, Capone's heirs, were the guilty men. There was Frank the Enforcer Nitti; Paul Ricca; Little New York Campagna; Phil D'Andrea; Frank Maritote (a relative of the Capones); Charles 'Cherry Nose' Gioe; John Rosseli; Ralph Pierce, the Camel's personal assistant; and, to lend the holding of the trial in New York some local colour perhaps, Louis Kaufman, the union's business manager in Newark, New Jersey. '. . . the worst blow in the history of the mob', reported Edwin A. Lacey from New York on 19 March 1943 as the federal grand jury handed down the indictments.

The mob has sunk its roots deep in the social structure of Chicago in the past 20 years with only sporadic harassment by the local law. This worst blow has come about because the mobsters came to New York to make a few touches and thus put themselves in the jurisdiction of simple-minded authorities who operate on the theory that it is a punishable crime to steal money and shake people down.

NITTI, CAMPAGNA AND RICCA ACCUSED IN $2,500,000 UNION
RACKETS: 27-YEAR TERMS POSSIBLE ran a headline that March day,
read with general approval. If there was jealousy in Chicago
that their boys were being tried in New York and even some
feeling that it was none of New York's business – didn't they
have their own, if lesser, hoodlums in the East? – there was
formal pleasure that these Capone princes would be put
away. Only among very small groups in Chicago and on the
West Coast, distinguished though they might be, did the
extent of the indictments cause astonishment. They understood the reason why the people arrested had been, but
where, asked the politicians, the minor hoods, the specialist
journalists in trade union and bombing affairs, the entertainers,
the judges, where was the man himself? The master-corrupter,
the fixer, Capone's first inheritor, Llewelyn Morris
Humphreys, Murray the Camel? Was there a misprint?
Had the press missed out a name?

The propaganda from the New York District Attorney's
office had been such that the public was convinced that the
Outfit had been arraigned as a result of unprecedented bril-
liance and courage in detection. If that was the case, as the
leading Chicago mob-watchers, Art Petaque among them,
saw it, than clearly Humphreys must be on the list. Hadn't he
been poor, murdered Maloy's 'advisor' back in the thirties in
the early days, one of Bioff's oldest acquaintances, often seen
in Beverly Hills when his arrested colleagues were not? Many
years later it became clear that the prosecution case must have
rested far more heavily on the Bioff testimony than on any
intrepid conduct by New York's legal legmen. Bioff had
chosen not to name Humphreys along with the other con-
spirators, therefore an indictment would not hold up against
the Camel. That Bioff's motive was simply that this particular prince was a gentleman, was so well-regarded, was held
in such affection, did not become clear either until much later.
Only in the late fifties did the FBI become convinced that
the reason Bioff would not give evidence against Humphreys
so that the Welshman would be indicted along with his
colleagues really was that simple: the Camel was held in too
high a regard, was such an unusual gentleman. Bioff did not
want to be responsible for Humphreys going to jail.

There was one arcane, if low, sense in which it might have been unfair if Humphreys had been arrested with the certainty of conviction on this particular charge. His policy was to keep sources of cash and its distribution as closely under control as was commensurate with the fact that their acts were villainous. He could scarcely have approved of money arriving in Chicago *via* New York and certainly not by any method which permitted the authorities to know that it was passing through town. It's unlikely that the Camel was aware of the shrewd advice given and always followed by a more respectable Welsh political genius, David Lloyd George – although Lloyd George was for a long time the most popular foreign statesman in the United States: never neglect your constituency. Humphreys often carried large sums himself, just as often under an alias or wearing a disguise, to ensure that a congressman in Washington or a state senator or a colleague received his reward discreetly. But no one could lay a finger on the cash or him. Certainly it would be foreign to him to have any city but Chicago involved in any affairs by which he could be arraigned. He just didn't know enough policemen or politicians or judges in other American cities to feel the security which home gave him. To be tried in a New York court would, therefore, have been particularly disagreeable for him, offending his principles more profoundly perhaps than the experience did his colleagues! His long-standing Capone ally Frank the Enforcer Nitti, for example, would scarcely be as sensitive.

Or so it might have been thought. Yet as soon as he was indicted in New York Nitti, who had killed so many to maintain Al Capone's power, who once had had a police bullet rattling around in his head, shot himself. (Kenneth Allsop in *The Bootleggers* reports a rumour that Nitti had been murdered and his body found in a ditch, but the prevailing view is that it was suicide.) Why it should have happened is not clear. One school of thought is that Nitti was still depressed at the death of his wife in 1940: he had appeared in court with Humphreys in the Double Jeopardy Trial wearing a black suit and black tie. Another is that he simply could not face going to prison. How could the publicly recognised leader of the Outfit go to jail, and on a charge that was, relatively, of such small import?

For the Camel, Nitti's suicide created difficulties greater than the fact that so many of the mob leaders were likely to be in jail for a long time. Humphreys had spent some time – had even done time – to create an understanding whereby Nitti was treated as Capone's inheritor, as chairman. The public knew him; the law-enforcement officers knew him. In partnership they had prospered, had used the past decade wisely to move away from mere slaughter in the streets to less evident but more secure business. No doubt there were times when they reminisced about the twenties, talked about the days then they would swing mayoral elections with the polemics of the machine gun, the persuasive arguments of the pineapple bomb, throwing acid along with ideological confusion – except, by many accounts, Nitti was not much given to talking: he just grunted agreement with, first, Capone and then Humphreys. Who would replace the Enforcer?

More immediately, how long would Ricca, Campagna, Rosseli, Gioe and the rest be put away for? The indictment was long and comprehensive. Essentially, though, it first repeated the charges on which Browne and Bioff had been convicted: demanding money from the Hollywood studios and 'restraining and impeding inter-state distribution and exhibition of motion pictures'. And then there were charges of malpractice in the IATSE union, among them that 2 per cent 'tariff' imposed on members for the benefit of the boys in Chicago. Those boys were found guilty as charged and sentenced to ten years in prison. And there was such relief that at last the Capone gang was bust. Al Capone, its founder, was now a vegetable, near death in Florida. Syphilis, caught in one of his own Cicero brothels, had reached his brain. Nitti was dead. The rest were inside – never, polite society had it, to resume their sway. One man in Chicago, far from any jail, shared neither the spirit of rejoicing nor despair: the Camel, as was his wont, was considering the landscape on the other side of the hill and how its contours could be used to his and the Outfit's advantage. He soon evolved a gambit which was to create quite as much fury in the United States as the jailing of his friends had created delight.

11   The disease as epidemic

Father did not have a great respect for politicians because he knew that he could control them. He even knew Harry Truman and at one time Mother and I were in Washington and Harry Truman showed us around. He became President of the United States shortly afterwards.

Llewella Humphreys, in conversation, 1983

What physicians say about disease is applicable here: that at the beginning a disease is easy to cure but difficult to diagnose; but as time passes, not having been recognised or treated at the outset, it becomes easy to diagnose but difficult to cure. The same thing occurs in affairs of state; for by recognising from afar the diseases that are spreading in the state (which is a gift given only to the prudent ruler), they can be cured quickly; but when they are not recognised and are left to grow to the extent that everyone recognises them, there is no longer any cure.

Niccolò Machiavelli, *The Prince*, 1532

In Humphreys' day, after Capone, the Outfit in Chicago always had a corporate structure – and I want to debunk those myths in the movies like the Godfather and the Cosa Nostra: that's all bunkum. In Chicago we had every ethnic group – except minority types. We had no blacks: the gentlemen were not in favour of equal opportunity. So there would be ten people on the board of the Outfit and Humphreys would have the floor more often than anybody else. Accardo would be the chairman,

Gusik the vice-chairman and Humphreys would be the
president.

Art Petaque, *Chicago Sun-Times*,
in conversation, 1983

With Nitti dead and the others in jail for who knew how
long, the Outfit considered how best to present themselves,
both to each other and to the world. Humphreys at the age
of forty-four was now the important figure among the
survivors of the twenties battles. Anthony Accardo was
seven years younger, so was Joseph Aiuppa; Jake Gusik, if
older, took orders: the Outfit were wise enough not to give
their accountant power. None of these was anxious to seize
the limelight. There was also Paul Ricca's position to be
considered, as the senior man inside.

Among the younger men there was one whom Humphreys
is held to have encouraged in this awkward period, in Mike
Royko's words 'an unknown semi-literate until Humphreys
made him a well-known semi-literate'. This was Sam
Giancanna, who was to come to want to be known as the
leader, and to infuriate his mentor by his ostentation.
Giancanna had been charged with three murders before
he was twenty and was to be shot down, ten years after
Humphreys had died of a heart attack. The second to be
advanced was Joey Glimco, a more senior, if obscure figure
whom the Camel is thought to have introduced to his friend
Jimmy Hoffa: certainly Glimco became the boss in Chicago
of Hoffa's important Teamsters' Union and the city's taxi
cabs. (One story goes that the taxi drivers tried to break away
and join with men working the river and Lake Michigan, at
which Hoffa asked if they thought their taxis would float,
and had many thrown into the Chicago River.)

If the gang seemed in trouble in 1943 and 1944, the Welshman was observed by friends and family to be cheerful. He
was at the height of his profession. The Second World War
was being fought far from Chicago. He travelled around
America more than he had been accustomed to do. He proposed to buy a house in Florida across the water from Cuba
so that he could more easily go deep-sea fishing, which was
an enthusiasm of his. 'I used to go fishing with him,' his

daughter told me, 'because he was such a busy man, if I wanted to spend a lot of time with him, I had to do the things he loved doing and he loved deep-sea fishing. I used to do all the things with him that a son would have done. I used to go hunting with him, too.' Her mother by this period was playing a unique part in the transactions of the Outfit. No other woman, before or since, has been privy to the secrets of the mob. Her unusual memory enabled her to keep their financial transactions in her head. Nothing was written down: Mrs Humphreys would simply remember. And, for all that the 'gentlemen' were unfortunately in the cooler, Hollywood was still available to the charming Camel and his family.

He also began looking for land in Oklahoma, for a hunting lodge where he could both shoot the wild animals of the territory and enjoy his interest in birds, exotic in that otherwise uncelebrated state. He was determined to build his own house and he did. It still stands, modest, with a small porch, crowded by the trees he planted, its carpentry – hickory from round about, American oak – sound, even, in the carved chairs, expert. The countryside around was, when I was there, dry, red and dusty, undulating, the rough roads marked by shanties where poor Indians lived. Winter brings snow and damp cold. Mrs Humphreys was part Indian: her daughter has recently married one. There are three small oil wells on the estate which looked to be self-operating. At night the mountain lions and coyotes keep you awake until their noise becomes familiar. The Camel was much taken by the fact that many of the bolder bank robberies conducted by Bonnie and Clyde took place only a few miles down the road, but thought the pair stupid to have been caught: he seems to have had no romantic Celtic instinct for self-destruction, however much he might have wished, in his heart, to resign from his criminal trade.

His travels, it soon became clear, were not always so uxorious, familial and innocent. Who knows which alias he used? Lewis Hunt was one, indeed many of them had the initials L.H., probably because it was useful to have those matching the initials he was christened with and used on his luggage. Quite where he took the train to is uncertain: the scholars in the Loop, when the new drama developed, thought St Louis, Kansas City, maybe Los Angeles, certainly Washington to see Vice-President Truman who was so delighted to meet the Humphreys family. Not that it was quite clear why the Camel should be so friendly with former Senator Harry S. Truman: the latter had nothing to do with Chicago. On the other hand the Democratic boss Prendergast who ran Kansas and his machine which had elected Senator Truman had behaved in the Chicago mode, had emulated its wide-open style in the twenties, had encouraged jazz as much as the Chicago speakeasies ever did. Even so, the relationship had an unlikely air about it in an America where the separate city states had, traditionally, seldom concerned themselves with each other.

When the storm broke in Washington in August 1947 and Americans began to be aware that Machiavelli's 'disease' was truly about in the land, Humphreys was elsewhere, indeed was occupied in conjuring up a new virus in Nevada in his usual insouciant manner which was, as ever, to lead to his survival and the murder of his better-known associates. The Loop aficionados, when the curtains were lifted, could detect that Humphreys did not need President Truman's help to produce this new drama, even if it did brush the White House: the evidence was that he had fixed it in his own home territory, the Democratic First Ward of Chicago, in the Loop itself.

The storm broke over the release from jail, on parole, of the Chicago mob after serving only three years of their sentences. The public was incredulous. How could this be? Hadn't this sinister bunch of hoods been put away to break the corrupting powers of the Outfit? And for ever at that? Only six months before, in February, Al Capone himself had been buried in Chicago, four of his old comrades (Humphreys among them) with the family at the graveside. So why should the Justice Department in Washington decide to allow Ricca, Campagna, Gioe, Rosseli and the rest to emerge from their appropriate prisons in Kansas and Missouri and walk free? It was unheard of for convicted men to be allowed out after serving less than a third of their sentences. Why make an exception for gangsters? Why indeed?

The Justice Department had heard many pleas. Little New York Campagna, for example, a man who had once surprised Chicago by pulling a gun on the police chief at his headquarters, was supported by the Catholic priest Father M. A. Canning:

I have known Campagna and particularly his family for fifteen years. There are three young daughters just growing to womanhood. One of them is a student at Rosary College. His boy Joe was in the Air Corps and was quite a hero just when his father was going to prison. They promised me with tears in their eyes that he would be a good citizen if he was let out.

Father Canning's supplications and those of the presidents of trucking, construction and minor newspaper companies in Chicago were not, in the enraged public response, thought to carry as much weight as the lawyer who appeared for the hoods. He was none other than the former campaign manager for President Truman when he had been running for the Senate: a St Louis lawyer named Paul Dillon. The president's Republican opponents grew almost demented when they further discovered that Attorney Dillon had also defended John Nick and Clyde Weston – as it happens, at Murray Humphreys' request – when both were IATSE union officers in St Louis and were caught thumping movie theatre owners in 1939. The House of Representatives decided to form a committee to investigate this supposedly unprecedented scandal, the first of many such helpless, solemn enquiries. The parole decisions were to have serious consequences for American society; were to change a nation's understanding of itself, for those who cared to face its implications; were to promote cynicism more publicly; were to show that gangsters were part of the Federal Union: in an odd way, were to demonstrate that after a war in which the nation had fought together, there was a fresh genuine connection between its distant cities and states, if only because corruption united them. Chicago spoke to Washington and Washington answered: Yes. In the meantime the comedies associated with the hoods' release occupied as much space in press and broadcasting as concerns about Soviet policy, about Winston Churchill's Fulton concept of the Iron Curtain, about the Marshall Plan. How could any schemes of Moscow's compare with the achievements of Chicago?

Mayor Kennelly and Chief of Police Prendergast warned the freed gangsters to keep away from their old stamping-ground. Said the mayor: 'We don't want any except law-abiding citizens in Chicago. I have directed my policemen to pick these men up whenever they see them in the streets.' Ricca and Campagna responded by saying that they intended to be gentlemen farmers, far from the Loop. D'Andrea thought he might become a steel salesman.

The House of Representatives' committee was to jive to as lively a dance by the Outfit's tune as to any jazz played by the Mezzrows, Armstrongs, Beiderbeckes or Goodmans in the hoods' haunts at home. Republican congressmen Hoffman from Michigan and Busby from Illinois, who knew quite well what was going on in the famous First Ward in the Windy City, who were familiar with the history of the Bath and Hinky Dink and their faithful heirs, did all they could to reveal it. They re-arrested Campagna and Ricca and D'Andrea for breaking parole by resuming their old work. It did no good. They complained that the hoods had done a deal with the Income Tax on their illegal earnings, paying in some cases only a quarter of a million dollars when they owed a million. The Revenue wearily suggested that half or even a quarter of a loaf was better than no bread; and anyway the US Supreme Court had ruled that 'embezzled funds are not subject to income tax': did extorted funds meet that proviso?

In 1950 the United States Senate reluctantly turned its head towards the scandal of the mob's parole and its implications. Senator Estes Kefauver, who had expressed his concern as a young lawyer in Tennessee at a possible tie-up, as he put it, between organised crime and politics, became Chairman of the Senate Crime Investigating Committee and between May 1950 and May 1951 travelled the States interrogating witnesses. He discovered little from the Chicago heavies who had been house trained by Humphreys. But what some of the Outfit's helpers let slip astonished him and his Counsel

Halley. In passing the committee had condemned the parole given the mobsters, granted 'against the recommendations of the prosecuting attorney and of the judge who had presided at their trial. In the opinion of this committee, this early release from imprisonment of three dangerous mobsters is a shocking abuse of parole powers.' Its coloquy with the lawyer who helped the gangsters to arrange their tax payments to meet the government's demands equally had the committee enraged.

Eugene Bernstein had been an Inland Revenue officer. He studied law in his spare time and acquired a law licence. From time to time he acted as a lawyer for Murray Humphreys and through him for Accardo and Guzik. He had never acted for the imprisoned Ricca or Campagna until, mysteriously, he was called in to settle their tax affairs and so help along their release from jail. He began to make trips to Leavenworth Prison in Accardo's company to see the hoods, having, he claimed, met Accardo by chance. It seemed the mobster just walked into his office one day and offered to help settle the matter of Ricca's and Campagna's tax.

COUNSEL HALLEY: 'It just doesn't sound like something I can visualise . . . Who walks in but a notorious gangster, and he tells you, "I am the man" and you accept that without checking back?'
BERNSTEIN: 'I never knew Mr Accardo to be a notorious gangster, sir, at that time, nor do I know him to be a gangster now.'

Bernstein, with Accardo's help, was able to persuade the reluctant gangsters that they had to pay some tax and a settlement was reached and the money paid – although the lawyer testified that he never knew where the money came from. Strangers would just drop by at his office and leave cash with his secretary, some $190,000 in all. In the course of his evidence to the commission, Eugene Bernstein made what Senator Kefauver called a 'spirited defence' of Murray Humphreys, claiming that the Welshman had been 'forced' out of a legitimate laundry business because of 'political activities'.

Counsel Halley: 'What do you mean "political activities"?'
Bernstein: 'I mean because he tried to go into legitimate business and was not permitted to.'
Counsel Halley: 'Why not?'
Bernstein: 'Just because of the newspapers and other people that kept pushing him around.'

Senator Kefauver and his colleagues were surprised by this view of Murray the Camel as a pathetic, put-upon businessman striving for respectability. But many of the opinions expressed by Attorney Bernstein, the ex-Revenue man, seemed to take them aback. For example:

Bernstein: 'The word "gangster" has a different connotation to me than it may have to other people. A gangster is an individual who by means of force, duress, obtains sums of money. If you and I go out and do certain things legally, and place funds in his possession without duress, at our own direction, and he does something with that, that would not be gangsters. Gangsterism is a very definite form of violence.'
Counsel Halley: 'A gangster is a man who belongs to a gang, isn't he?'
Bernstein: 'Then you and I are gangsters . . .'
Halley: 'What gang do you belong to?'
Bernstein: 'We belong to the human race. We belong to a political party. That may be a gang.'

The granting of the paroles to the gentlemen of the Outfit had one small effect in Chicago. When the congressmen discovered that money had been the root of their release, that members of the Democratic party in the Chicago First Ward had 'reached' people empowered to grant parole, that some half a million dollars had been available, in response the wise men of the First Ward, guided by the Camel, made some changes. Peter Fosco, their head, was thought to be embarrassed that one of his sidekicks had been named as a man who passed the bribe. Fosco went to Washington as a national officer of the Plumbers' Union and was replaced in the Loop by Frank Annunzio, soon to be appointed State Director of Labour by Governor Adlai Stevenson. For Murray Humphreys all this commotion had been the preoccupation of two years ago. He had moved on, carrying with him the perception that nothing was now impossible, that Washington was not all that far away; more, that he had once again astonished his colleagues, so much so that he need never witness anything horrible in the course of his business. It had been a long, long time since he had shot anyone. He was certain he would never need to, whatever other people might do.

12 Vegas, the Senate and Eisenhower

[The great man] knows he is incommunicable: he finds it tasteless to be familiar; when one thinks of it he usually is not. When not speaking to himself he wears a mask. He rather lies than tell the truth; it requires more spirit and will. There is a solitude within him that is inaccessible to praise or blame, his own justice that is beyond appeal.

Nietzsche, *The Will to Power*

I went into the room [in 1952] and there were four gentlemen of the Outfit there with my father and another man. One of the gentlemen said to me: 'What do you think of Dwight D. Eisenhower?' I said I'd vote for him if I could, to be the next President of the United States. The man next to me said: 'Thank you very much young lady.' It was General Eisenhower. I felt very small but I hadn't recognised him without his uniform.

Five men there in a room in Chicago decided who was going to be the next President of the United States.

Llewella Humphreys, in conversation, 1983

For decades the Outfit had made money from illegal gambling in Chicago, and such profits as escaped them usually went, one way or another, into supporting the Democratic party machine in the city; the cash might not go directly into party coffers, but more often into the pockets of those whose job it was to bring out the vote, or to dishonest cops: all contributions were welcome. Murray Humphreys had become more and more impressed at the fashion in which it

116

was easier to make money out of respectable booze than it
had been violently in Prohibition days. The manner in which
he had divided up legitimate business with Joseph Kennedy
in gin, whisky and beer created, in his mind, a precedent. He
now seldom saw the former Ambassador to the Court of
St James, although he did a few times take his wife and
daughter to meet the old man and his sons Jack and Bobby.
(He thought, according to Llewella, that Joe Kennedy
dominated the children too much; they were growing up
'wimps'.) With his usual clarity of analysis and consequent
action which with hindsight seems so obvious, Humphreys
considered that the next human weakness to be legalised
must be gambling. It was just as well for the United States
that the Camel had moral objections to exploiting narcotics
and prostitution. Or perhaps not.

The choice of the State of Nevada as the territory for the ex-
periment might not have seemed wise. It was far from everywhere, except California. However, it had the virtue that no
mobs were established. Flying was becoming fashionable.
Given the Outfit's command of night clubs and restaurants in
Chicago and Humphreys' continuing role in the Hollywood
unions, it shouldn't be difficult to lay on entertainment of
the highest quality in the Nevada desert. More, Humphreys
had so many hundreds of thousands of dollars to invest, to
launder somehow, that building a new city or two could
prove a useful front; and when had anyone gone broke cater-
ing for human folly? A persuasive factor was that there didn't
seem to be any other state in the USA which would lend
itself so easily to creating a safe, legal haven for the gambler.

The FBI now believes that the Camel went to Los Angeles
in 1946 with the prominent New York gangster Benjamin
'Bugsy' Siegel. William Roemer, the agent who pursued the
Camel, told me: 'He then switched to Las Vegas from Los
Angeles in 1947 and 1948, at the very beginning, just when
Las Vegas was getting started. He offered his counsel, as
usual. He made his investments on behalf of the Chicago
Outfit. But he did more than that. Because of his leadership
in organised crime throughout the country, he advised all the
gangsters throughout America on their investments, but of
course, his loyalty was always to Chicago.' Humphreys was

117

soon to be supported by John Rosseli, once the latter had been paroled prematurely, and by Meyer Lansky who, like Siegel, Rosseli and Sam Giancanna was to be murdered, probably by comrades. Indeed of all the mobsters involved in the creation of Las Vegas and the world-wide empire which grew from it, Humphreys alone was in life to be at liberty and to die peacefully. The notoriety of the others became universal and many singers and actors, presidents and trade union leaders, became embroiled in gossip about connections with them. Humphreys, although part-owning two of the most glamorous hotel-casinos, did not figure in any gossip.

The Outfit's role and profit in Nevada being established, Humphreys returned to Chicago where he was quickly involved, as anonymously as ever, in charity work and high politics. Siegel, Lansky and, soon, Giancanna could handle the gambling: he seems not to have concerned himself directly in its expansion to Cuba, where the dictator Batista was to be a pawn, to Beirut and, almost, to Teheran. (Giancanna is held to have messed up the negotiations with the shah.) The Camel, it was discovered when he died, had always given large sums of money to good causes. Such generosity is not unusual among the rich in America: what is unusual and made Humphreys, in the opinion of many, unique, is that he never set his gifts against tax. Those puzzled by this purity have wondered if his behaviour was due to his not wanting to attract notice to his tax position. The argument does not stand, since he always declared some income, however small a percentage it might have been of his true rewards, to the authorities. Nietzsche, the German philosopher quoted at the head of this chapter, offers another possible explanation in his *Beyond Good and Evil*: 'The noble man also helps the unfortunate not (or scarcely) out of sympathy, but rather out of an impulse produced by the superabundance of power.' It may be that the Camel was troubled by guilt; or that he just liked to help: he certainly never spoke of seeing himself as Robin Hood or, rather, the Welsh equivalent Twm Shon Catti.

For years he had been involved in raising funds for a camp for poor children in Chicago in which his favourite tame congressman, Roland V. Libonati (he of the riotous victory in 1930) had an interest. Even in 1960 the FBI were reporting that Humphreys was leaning on the Teamsters' Union asking for money for this camp, reminding them of how much Libonati had helped them in Washington. In 1951, however, Humphreys conceived a bold fund-raising scheme. He had seen to it that the relationship between Chicago, Hollywood and Las Vegas was close. Therefore he would ask those entertainers common to all three places if they would care to offer their services for a 'Night of Stars' in Chicago.

Since the charity was designed mainly to help Italian–American children the arrangements might more properly have been left to the Italian members of the Outfit – Accardo, Ricca, Giancanna and their juniors. They were lying low as, for much of the time, were the equally senior but non-Italian Gus Alex and Jake Guzik. Senator Estes Kefauver's committee investigating organised crime was still wrestling with the Parole Affair: someone, if not the whole mob, was sure to be indicted. It was true that Humphreys' record had been read out to the Senate Committee in Washington in June 1950 by V. W. Paterson, but the Camel was behaving with the air of a man who knew something the others did not.

So: here was this kindly sentiment: how to present it? The ideal place was the Chicago Stadium, holding tens of thousands of people. Bold though Humphreys might be he could scarcely, either alone or in the company of Giancanna, Accardo and the rest, approach City Hall and ask permission to hire the stadium. Not even Chicago's City Hall could hand over its pride and joy to the Outfit. Hinky Dink and the Bath might have managed it half a century earlier, but this was a big town now and the world was a smaller place: the word would get around. The answer was simple: the First Ward would arrange it. John D'Arco and Frank Annunzio were friendly. They could arrange it through the Democratic party and City Hall. And so it came to be that the people of Chicago in 1951 and in the following two years had glorious concerts at which Jimmy Durante, Frank Sinatra, Tony Martin, Bob Hope, Dean Martin, Tony Bennett and many more of the most celebrated of entertainers performed. If anyone turned down an invitation, the names have not been recorded. In the real world the origins of the occasion were known.

The proceeds were handed over to the camp for the poor.

There were no rake-offs. The members of the Outfit invariably maintain that in their dealings away from 'work' they were honest men. In 'work' a different kind of ethic might obtain. Art Petaque, a scholar with first-hand experience of the field, and a man scornful of the cinema and other fictional representations of 'The Mafia', defined it to me as follows: 'Anyone who attempts to burglarise or attempts to hold up or abuse in any way a crime syndicate member is marked for death – though sometimes they are given a warning, depending on the circumstances. But usually what will happen is that they will be killed first and the warning will be the killing. The word is then spread as to the reason for the death.' The same warning is given to anyone offering information to police, FBI or Revenue. The inability to recognise that there might be a common, benign ethic available both in business and in private life is by no means peculiar to the gentlemen of the Outfit, or even to American business. Certainly the gentlemen grew angry when they came to believe that their good works had been mocked once in Chicago.

At the same time as they were organising the 'Night of Stars', Llewella Humphreys told me, her father and friends decided to spend millions of their own dollars on an act of charity. They would build a model block of flats and donate them to the city so that a few people, anyway, could move from the slums in which they themselves had been brought up. The flats were built but very soon it became evident that the work had been shoddy, the materials poor and incompetently used; the roof leaked, the plumbing didn't plumb; it became unsafe; the Outfit were, word of mouth had it, playing a cruel trick: weren't they ripping off enough?

Such remains the received account in Chicago of what happened in 1952. I tried out the story on my friend Studs Terkel, the chronicler both of the city and of the rest of the United States. His *Hard Times, Working* and *Division Street America*, recording his conversations with his fellow countrymen, are necessary reading to try to begin to understand the place. So, in the small company at his hilarious seventy-third birthday party in 1983 in the L'Escargot restaurant in his home city I raised the matter: Studs would know what the people of Chicago remembered of the affair. He recalled it as a mob fiasco. I then passed on the version Llewella Humphreys had given me: he was astonished.

The story really was about the Governor of Illinois, Adlai Stevenson, a Democrat. He was hoping to be – and succeeded in being nominated – the party's candidate for the presidency in November 1952. Chicago was a Democrat stronghold. In 1948 there had been surprise that the crowd of ruffians in charge of the Democrat machine in the city, in Cook County, should have proposed Adlai Stevenson as governor since he was a man celebrated for intellect, charm and wit and was a known liberal. Cynics had it that they expected to lose the election and wished to enjoy a worthy, even distinguished image without suffering the practical consequences of enlightenment. However, there he was, the nominee to succeed the Democrat President Harry S. Truman, and soon to be admired by liberals in Europe for his varied qualities. The Republicans had nominated General Dwight D. Eisenhower, hero of war and peace, a strong candidate but, given the power of the Democratic machine in important states, not a guaranteed winner. That machine was nowhere stronger or more experienced in the ways of voting than in Chicago and, in Chicago, than in the First Ward where Humphreys quietly held sway.

Llewella Humphreys takes up the tale: 'The gentlemen of the Outfit had invested a great deal of money in this scheme. They were doing it from the heart, not for profit. Adlai Stevenson's construction company got the contract. The houses were constructed and about a year after the tenants moved in they started crumbling. In other words everything was sub sub material. He had really cut corners, more than the normal graft. The gentlemen had been going to support Stevenson, but when they found this out, they changed sides. They decided to back Dwight D. Eisenhower. Father went to see him several times about his ideas and certain promises that would be kept. Then, when General Eisenhower met five gentlemen in Chicago, I was fortunate enough to walk in on the meeting.'

That such a story strikes the visitor as credible says much for United States or at least for Chicago politics. It is a serious matter for any candidate to lose such wealth in support of a campaign. In 1960, when the Outfit had returned to the Democrats in order to support the son of their old sparring partner Joseph Kennedy, without some thousands of dubious votes cast in the First and neighbouring wards John F. Kennedy might well have lost to Richard Nixon. The spirit of the twenties still lived.

Not that this negotiation was Humphreys' only engagement in high politics in the early fifties, which were also his own early fifties: in his age as much as his behaviour he was very much a man of the American Century. He had appeared before the Senate Committee and astonished it and the public by pleading the Fifth Amendment. He was told he couldn't do that. He maintained he could. He was cited for contempt, appeared in court, when the United States government learned that indeed the Camel could. In 1958 when the Senate next attempted to break up the Outfit, while penalising colleagues Accardo and Giancanna, the decision was taken not to bother Humphreys. Why, no one knew. Perhaps they feared he had some new trick up his sleeve which would make them look ridiculous in a fresh fashion.

Those who knew him believe he would have been just as capable in the majestic surroundings of the Senate on Capitol Hill of the behaviour in 1959 which so awed a grand jury at the district Federal Court in Chicago. He had flown in from Arizona, by his account, or from his quarter-of-a-million-dollar house in Key Biscayne, Florida. In the latter palace he was known as Lewis Hart, a retired oil man: 'A gracious host, serving tall drinks at the swimming pool, chatting amiably about deep-sea fishing, giving to local charities in the manner of a man of affluence.' Wherever he had come from and wherever he was going, he presented a strange spectacle to the jury.

He wore a large black patch over one eye, much in the style of another Welsh pirate, Henry Morgan. His raincoat was crumpled and dirty. His shoes were scuffed. His homburg had seen better decades. He shuffled, supporting himself on a walking stick, pausing every few steps to breathe heavily and peer about him. 'Veteran court employees,' reported Norman Glubok in the *Chicago American*, 'and newspaper men, were moved as they contrasted this shell of a man with the Murray Humphreys they once had known, a vigorous and handsome man whose custom-tailored suits were always immaculate.' He was asked a few questions: he croaked the Fifth Amendment a few times. After five minutes the embarrassed court allowed him to leave. He shuffled into the April air, turned into Rush Street, threw away his walking stick, his raincoat and his homburg and skipped as blithely as ever from bar to bar to meet old friends. But the picture of the broken man was in every newspaper: the Camel, as one put it, was over the hump, manifestly finished. That he was as busy as ever and fit was not reported.

While these antics were being performed, Humphreys had divorced his wife Mary and had married Betty Jeanne Neibert, a former tavern dice-girl, pretty and twenty-five years younger than him. He was to leave her after six years and return to his first wife, saying: 'There's no fool like an old fool.' Before the divorce, his daughter Llewella had moved to Rome to study music. Her father had said that it would be a wonderful thing to be a concert pianist, so she decided that she would try to become one, as much to please him as herself: learning to play the piano that well, practising at least eight hours a day, must be one of the rarer forms of filial affection. Her childhood had been hard while privileged. To balance the riches and usually cheerful spirit at home were the torments at school. Children in class would imitate the sound of a machine gun and say: 'Your pop is going to get it next.' Police would take her out of school and take her to a distant precinct hoping thus to discover where her father was. It was a fine thing to have Frank Sinatra come to her small high school graduation party and have his picture taken with each of them: 'He was very thin then and good-looking and very nice.' The obverse was the hounding by the press, for all her father's efforts at privacy and disguise. His sense of irony, if endearing, was also confusing: for example, his joke in building her a doll's house in the garden so that it stood crookedly. She changed her name from Llewella to Louella, did become a pianist and gave three concerts with the Rome Symphony Orchestra. But Murray Humphreys could not travel to Italy out of fear that he would not be allowed to return to America. She retired so he never heard her play in the concert hall.

13 Gang murder, number one thousand

Anyone, therefore, who will carefully examine the actions of this man [Emperor Severus] will find him a very ferocious lion and a very shrewd fox; and he will see him feared and respected by everyone and not hated by his armies; and one should not be amazed that he, a new man, was able to hold so great an empire; for his outstanding reputation always defended him from that hatred which the common people could have for him on account of his plundering.

Niccolò Machiavelli, The Prince, 1532

Anything my father wanted, he had; but it was given, not demanded. It was given in homage. He had power, absolute power, more than you can find in the big corporations, because he and his people were into every facet of business. And once the old days were over, they didn't have to threaten any more because they had the power. Let's face it, they were respected for achieving the position they had.

Llewella Humphreys, in conversation, 1983

The statistics of murder between gangs or within gangs in Chicago are not quite reliable. Is it fair to include the girlfriends of hoods shot in the course of revenge? There is general agreement, however, that as 1959 drew to its close the figure for the past forty years stood somewhere between 990 and 998, a figure which excludes policemen or bystanders. There had been seventeen indictments which came to court. There had been two convictions. The days of savagery, it was understood, were long gone, murder no more the invention of necessity. Commentators were remarking on the staid gait of corruption but, as it turned out, prematurely. Four days before Christmas 1959 Roger Tuohy (see Chapter 8) was shot down and the press, television and radio of the United States was able to revive for Yuletide study the saga of the Capone days: Murray Humphreys left town for the holidays.

If this assassination of one of the most prominent enemies of Al Capone attracted universal attention and may be counted as the thousandth such, number 999 four months earlier on 26 August held more importance both for members of the Outfit and for the authorities. On the morning of that day Frederick Evans was struck down by five bullets at the junction of Lotus Avenue and Lake Street. Evans was sixty years old. He had appeared in court along with Murray Humphreys in the McLane Affair in 1939 (see Chapter 9). Like the Camel, Evans had interests in the laundry business: the Linen of the Week Inc., Western Laundry Service, Infant Diaper Service, the Dust and Tex Cleaning Company and, the largest, the Industrial Garment Service. He also was part owner of two hotels in Los Angeles. Three of his safety deposit boxes were found holding half a million dollars in cash. One report has it that a piece of paper was found in his safe on which was written 'Total resources $11 million', but it was not clear if this was accountant Evans' private fortune or that of his collaborators.

Frederick Evans was known to be a servant of Murray Humphreys. His death revealed that he also shared some of his companies with Joey Glimco and, further, that Glimco and the Camel were engaged together in several commercial enterprises. There were hidden interests in record and jukebox companies, in importing motor cars: only four years later did the investigators discover that Glimco and Humphreys had relatives on the pay roll of a construction company which received contracts for $4 million from City Hall. What, then, had disturbed such a long-standing and profitable business relationship, one which also enabled Evans to live as a well-regarded citizen? Or, rather, a citizen who had never been to jail? It could hardly be that along with Tony Accardo, Sam Giancanna and Joey Glimco (but not Humphreys) Evans had been subpoenaed in an enquiry into a bout of rough-housing in the unions.

The answer lay in an investigation being conducted into Teamster Joey Glimco by the Internal Revenue Service. The IRS was particularly interested in the income from the Industrial Garment Service. The Outfit was sensitive at this time about income tax since their colleague Paul Ricca was serving ten years in the Terre Haute Penitentiary in Indiana for tax offences. (The following year, 1960, according to the FBI, Humphreys was to arrange for Congressman Roland Libonati to visit Ricca in jail, with the result that Ricca was to serve only two out of his ten-year sentence.) The Outfit was led to believe that Evans was telling all to the Revenue and a little to the FBI about labour racketeering. So he died and Glimco was the principal suspect but was not arrested: no one was.

For the public the murder of a bureaucrat, the leaden handshake, if distressing as a comment on the affairs of Chicago, lacked glamour. How different the death of Tuohy and the revelations which followed it. Here was a man who had stood up to the fabulous Al Capone himself, who had defied the mob and maintained his own, independent bootlegging business through the fabulous epoch, even though four of his brothers were to be shot down. Towards the end of November 1959 he returned to Chicago, paroled after serving twenty-five years of his ninety-nine-year sentence for the kidnapping of Jake 'the Barber' Factor. He published his memoirs, *The Stolen Years*. The book presents the author as being a good man, his only crime running booze illegally which could, in the twenties, be held to be a public service. It offers an informed view about the assassination of Mayor Cermak when he stood alongside President Roosevelt in Biscayne Park, Florida in 1933. The bullet which killed was fired not from the gun of an anarchist who was believed to have aimed to shoot the president but by a member of the Outfit intent on removing a mayor elected as an enemy of the mob.

Of more interest to those survivors of Prohibition in

Chicago, whether public officials, journalists or gangsters, were to be his accounts of the kidnapping for which he was jailed and his pen-portraits of protagonists. He maintained that the Capone mob had framed him. That he, not being a kidnapper, would never have seized Jake the Barber Factor. Factor, therefore, must have been in cahoots with the Capone Syndicate. The Federal Court appeared to support this judgment at his parole. Roger the Terrible Tuohy then proceeds to refer to Murray Humphreys as a 'pimp'.

Journalists in Chicago reading the book in December 1959 thought this last epithet tactless of Tuohy. It was well known that the Camel grew angry when anyone suggested that he had anything to do with pimping, as with narcotics. Art Petaque confirmed this to me in his office at the *Chicago Sun-Times*: they were 'no-nos'. Mr Petaque (in 1983) recalled the publication especially well since a friend of his helped Tuohy to write the book and subsequently blamed himself for the former gangster's death, believing that had it not been written Tuohy might have survived (revelations which followed the death made that improbable). He also recalled that a surprising number of people could remember where Humphreys had been on 21 December 1959 when the men with shotguns met Tuohy as he stepped from his sister's house. He was seen playing a hand of cards at a place on North Clark Street. He was seen at a table in a bar, his usual small whisky in front of him, with friends. (Humphreys always sat at a table, never at the bar, thus demonstrating that he was not a drinking man.) He was seen later at the fashionable restaurant Fritzel's. I was told at L'Escargot that Humphreys had also been in there that evening, but scholars doubt this. And, lo and behold, who should be eating that night just down the street at the Singapore but Jake Factor, no longer 'the Barber' but a rich financier from Beverly Hills, just flown into Chicago.

Naturally enough Murray Humphreys was suspected of being responsible for the murder although no one supposed he would have carried it out himself, having put that kind of dirty work behind him in his youth. A surprising number of people, anyway, were familiar with his alibi. Just as naturally, the publication of Tuohy's book provoked speculation about that kidnapping of Factor twenty-six years earlier. Had it not been the case that Humphreys had been sent by Capone, along with Sam Golf Bag Hunt, Machine Gun Jack McGurk and Louis Little New York Campagna, to try to negotiate with Tuohy in 1931? And wasn't he the only survivor of that formidable quartet? Odd, too, that Humphreys had been Public Enemy Number One at the time of the seizing – or not – of Factor, Capone by that time being in jail. And hadn't kidnapping been a tactic Humphreys above all was celebrated for practising? Delightful these questions might be to pose: they were not thought relevant to Tuohy's murder. There were many other suspects beside Humphreys, even though he had a particular motive in the libel against him. Rumour was strong that a small dissident group had approached Tuohy on his release from jail to re-employ his talents to try to break the monopoly power of the Outfit, to give someone else a look-in on the huge profits being made in America from the Chicago base.

Even had Tuohy survived to enjoy his first Christmas out of jail for a quarter of a century, a new interpretation offered at the turn of the year of events in 1931 would have ensured it was his last. The writer and sociologist Saul Alinsky, who had been a member of the Prison Board at Tuohy's prison in 1960, made startling claims for the gangster and his relationship with Mayor Cermak, claims which were not made in the memoirs. Received opinion had been that the mayor had been elected on a noble platform: he would drive the Capone mob out of Chicago. In passing, he was also to build up the Democratic machine into such a formidable instrument that it was to make corruption endemic and unshakable, but that was not clear at the time.

Saul Alinsky maintained that the true position was different. In the interests of the mayoral election the candidate had made a deal with Tuohy. Anton J. Cermak would lend Roger the Terrible his police force in order to launch an attack on Capone, if Tuohy would help in the mayoral election. This 'revisionist' interpretation dismayed Chicagoans who, looking down the dark caverns of the past, had believed that once upon a time they did elect a genuinely reforming soul to City Hall. On the other hand it would explain why Mayor Cermak was shot down standing along-side the Democrat President Franklin D. Roosevelt whom the Chicago machine had done so much to help elect. Not that President Roosevelt could have known that his party could disgrace itself with such a deal, surely? For the Outfit this fresh account, if true, held particular interest. In the gang warfare which followed the election of Mayor Cermak nearly all the hoods killed were members of the Capone gang; scarcely any of their rivals were shot. At one time Humphreys and Nitti were losing one soldier every day; they suffered ninety fatal casualties in the two years from 1931 to 1933: and in the latter year the mayor was shot, and Tuohy arrested for the Factor kidnap.

Did Capone, Humphreys and Nitti know of the Cermak–Tuohy deal in 1931? And if not, why not? The murder of the mayor, given it was their work, is not evidence of knowledge. It would be sufficient motive that they were excluded from the machine, and were still in some confusion at the ending of Prohibition with the new strategy not yet in place. The collapse of their regime at City Hall probably meant that political intelligence was not good. More conclu-sive is the argument that had they known, Tuohy is unlikely to have been framed for a kidnapping: he would have been shot. And it is even more certain that had they discovered Tuohy still alive in Chicago once they had heard Saul Alinsky's tale about just how their troops had been shot down in the early thirties, his days would have been num-bered. But he was dead for other reasons, anyway.

Tuohy's death was not to trouble Humphreys directly but to have consequences which created difficulties about income tax; and the difficulties about tax were to lead to him being associated with as nasty a murder as Chicago had known for a long time. The Internal Revenue became interested in a share deal between the Camel, or Curly as he was more usually known now, and the former Jake the Barber Factor. In 1960, after Tuohy's murder, Jake Factor sold Humphreys shares. He was attempting to gain control of the First National Life Insurance Company of America. To this end he was buying shares at $125 each. However the financier Mr Factor sold 400 shares to Mr Humphreys at $20 apiece. A few months later Mr Humphreys sold these shares back to Mr Factor at $125. Mr Humphreys had therefore made a capital profit of $42,000 without straining himself. What a mysterious transaction, thought the Internal Revenue. The FBI also were curious but, as ever, might just as well have tapped their heads against a brick wall.

The Revenue, like the FBI, continued their researches into the elder statesman of the Outfit. They asked him where he had found the money to buy the mansion in Florida since his income didn't seem to suggest he had been able to raise such a large sum in cash. They were also curious about his interest in a beer company which paid his friend Anthony Accardo (now regarded as the chairman of the Outfit) $75,000 a year in salary. They were not persuaded that he was retired, half-blind, frail, even if the public had been. Humphreys was untroubled. He explained that much of the money for the house in Key Biscayne had been given by his new wife Betty Jeanne when they had married six years earlier in 1957. To his astonishment he then discovered that the Revenue would not accept his statement. Why? Because his wife's former husband Irving Vine had offered to give evidence against him. His first piece of testimony had been that Betty Jeanne could not possibly have $50,000, as Humphreys had reported her gift to be.

Irving Vine in 1963 was fifty-nine years old. Murray Humphreys was sixty-four. His second wife, whom he was soon to leave, although he remembered her, as they say, in his will, was in her thirties. Therefore Vine could not have been jealous that she had left him for a younger man; cases of jealousy over an older, richer man are not uncommon. There is no firm evidence that Betty Jeanne had indeed 'left' Vine for Humphreys. However, Murray Humphreys was a mogul in the Outfit, the *non-pareil*. Vine had been only a bit-player, always barely making his way on the crumbs from the mighty, but a member of the gang for all that. Rules which obtained for the highest obtained for the lowest. Therefore there was consternation when it became known that Vine was helping the Revenue. And if against the Camel, who else? If it was jealousy, so virulent a form had not before been seen. When Willie Bioff had squealed in 1943 – and even he had not moved against the Camel – he had later been blown to eternity as his reward. The gentlemen of the Outfit called on Irving Vine to consider his position. Murray Humphreys suggested to him that he was being foolish and that no good would come of it. Harm would come of it – especially to Vine. Whichever strange god Vine was pursuing, he further informed the Revenue that his former wife never earned more than $75 a week, sustaining his evidence that she had not saved $50,000 while she was married to him: therefore the famous Murray Humphreys was telling them a pack of lies. Even after this betrayal friends high and low continued to visit Vine, urging him to consider his apostasy, these visits being taken as a sign that Humphreys was exhibiting a patience no other chieftain would have shown. Vine refused to listen. His was to be a dreadful martyrdom. It took place at the Del Prado Hotel in Hyde Park. The hotel was owned by Ralph Pierce, Humphreys' Irish assistant. Humphreys' parents had once lived there, free, in great comfort. Ovid Demaris, in his *Captive City*, has this account of the morning of 6 May 1963:

Rosie Mitchell a chambermaid noticed that the door to Room 507 was ajar. After a discreet knock, she stepped into the room, took one look, and stepped right out again, screaming. Homicide detectives found Irving Vine lying on the floor, dressed only in blood-smeared shorts, his mouth and nose sealed with surgical tape, his legs also bound with tape, a shirt twisted loosely around his neck, and a pillow covering his head. Three of his ribs were broken, his face was scratched and his knees bruised, but the real damage was to the lower part of his body where savage tortures had been inflicted with an ice-pick during a period of several hours. Death was due to suffocation, 'by person or persons unknown'. Police stated they would like to question Humphreys, Betty Jeanne, Gus Alex, Edward Vogel, Nathan 'Butch' Ladon, Bernard 'Pipi' Posner and Ralph Pierce, the hidden owner of the Del Prado Hotel. Betty Jeanne remained in Florida; Humphreys vacated his Chicago apartment and successfully avoided arrest by becoming a nomad for a few weeks.

Later Humphreys was to express his shock at what had happened, the implication being that he was not responsible for the behaviour of his troops or, rather, the Outfit's troops; the further implication being that Vine really had to go: otherwise where would the mob be, with satraps running to the Revenue? In 1963 this demand for loyalty was becoming more serious than ever; the assaults on the gang by the Revenue and the FBI were critically damaging. Indeed for the past five years, since 1958, the Outfit had needed to contend with a new force against them: Robert Kennedy. Through the Senate and as attorney general when his brother Jack became president in 1961, Bobby Kennedy had set his sights on the Outfit. Humphreys was the principal target. The Camel found this wry, having been an old rival of the brothers' father and having, as the Chicago mob thought, helped to arrange President Kennedy's election. It was to be a battle to many deaths.

14 The Camel and the Kennedys

When Robert Kennedy took action against the Syndicate it was a turning point for my father and the organisation, a time of great pressure. Before that any information that was gleaned was either from the precincts or from a city. They, like a state or a county, or the FBI, had different pieces of evidence. If anyone tried to put all this information together to try to get something on someone it might take a year or two. Bobby Kennedy came along and put a central computer in Washington to which everything went. It really was a problem for the gentlemen of the Outfit. He stepped on some toes did Bobby Kennedy and there was a lot of talk about how to remedy the situation.
Llewella Humphreys, in conversation, 1983

Had I known about Murray Humphreys at the time, what would I have done with the knowledge? In May 1963 I was in the Oval Office at the White House with President Kennedy and his brother Robert★. We talked about unemployment in West Virginia and Kentucky where I had just spent a couple of weeks filming. Humphreys the brainy hood I knew of only as an unlikely Welsh legend. But if I had realised that the brothers' father Joe had been a rival in the old days, would I

★I was there to help to arrange the first live BBC satellite television broadcast between the USA and the United Kingdom. President Kennedy was awarding an honour to Sir Winston Churchill whose son Randolph was receiving it on his father's behalf. The pioneer pictures of the ceremony in the Rose Garden arrived perfectly in London. The familiar line carrying my sound commentary broke down.

have said anything? Or had I known that Robert, both as a Senate counsel and as attorney general had a special loathing for the Welshman and had been foiled so often in his pursuit, might I have asked why it was that Humphreys was so elusive when other mobsters had been jailed? That the gossip was that the mob had been involved in the Cuban Bay of Pigs fiasco; even that the CIA were looking for its help in assassinating Fidel Castro? What delicate form of words could be found to ask if it were true that Humphreys had invested in the West Virginia primary where victory was so important to the then Senator John F. Kennedy? And, further, that the ten thousand votes whereby Chicago and Illinois swung to Kennedy against Richard Nixon and so took him to the White House, were more or less fraudulently arranged by the master fixer?

In retrospect, it would have been a good time to have raised the subject since the Camel had recently helped to engineer an exceptional *coup* in Congress through his good friend Roland Libonati. On the ground that the civil rights of citizens – namely themselves and fellow hoods throughout the nation – were being infringed by the wire-tapping of the mob's meetings, the attorney general had been instructed to stop the practice. This was popularly known as the 'James Hoffa resolution' since it was partly in aid of Hoffa, the President of the Teamsters' Union and a Humphreys protégé, who had complained that Attorney General Kennedy was persecuting him. In a memorable if meaningless phrase Hoffa had cried at Kennedy: 'Sticks and stones may break my bones but words are only yesterday's whispers.' In retrospect, equally, the speculation is otiose: I did not know about Humphreys, not even enough to travel to Chicago to try to meet him, if only for a chat about the old country.

In considering the relationship between the Camel and the Kennedy family, therefore, hearsay, federal wire-taps, often persuasive gossip and the evidence of such court appearances as the attorney general could persuade Humphreys to make, have to compensate for any direct testimony. The matter is made more complicated because Humphreys in the relevant period from 1958 to the murder of President Kennedy in Dallas in 1963 had placed Sam Giancanna in the limelight.

That Giancanna's behaviour infuriated the Camel is known, nevertheless in the FBI wire-tapping files it is the fatally vain Italian who does most of the enraged shouting against the Kennedys. Humphreys' technique to deal with the FBI's eavesdropping was to open the meetings of the Syndicate by announcing briskly that the session had begun, and then remove the microphone. He also acquired a telescope which he would train on any agents who were watching out for him. Nevertheless there are records of some of his deals, especially at Las Vegas when he was engaged in removing millions of dollars from hotels there in the early sixties.

In 1958 Robert F. Kennedy let it be known that he was determined to attack the Outfit or Syndicate, recognising that it was a more serious disease in the society even than the Mafia. His particular enemy was Murray Humphreys, followed by Anthony Accardo, Gus Alex, Sam Giancanna and Jimmy Hoffa. Kennedy was the chief counsel of the Senate 'Rackets' committee or, to give it its full title, the US Senate Select Committee on Improper Activities in the Labour or Management Field. In turn the mobsters appeared before the Senate committee and pleaded the Fifth Amendment; Hoffa was taken to court, but was acquitted; Accardo was taken to court and convicted of income tax evasion. Humphreys never even appeared before the Senate committee. Kennedy could not find the means to serve a subpoena on the Welshman. No one is able to explain why this should be. How could it come about – as in the Hollywood trial – that the one man everyone in the know knew was peculiarly relevant to any investigation of the rackets in modern times simply strolled away from a summons to a Senate hearing? In the Hollywood case it was that he was too much admired by his colleagues to be shopped. Surely it could not be the position that no agent of federal law could be found to carry out so distasteful a task? Perhaps it was that he had quite persuaded everyone by his antics in other courts that he was retired, or sick; a feeble figure of no account.

This is improbable since at this time the FBI agent William Roemer was meeting Humphreys frequently in Chicago. Roemer's first meeting with the Camel (see Chapter 1) had impressed the young officer. He had complained about his

135

children being harassed at school by hoods from the Syndicate. Humphreys had listened politely and returned to assure the FBI man that such behaviour would stop, proposing that each side behaved with courtesy towards the other. Here was the Camel, as ever, conducting himself as if he were some plenipotentiary from a rival state within the state. No doubt that is how he saw his role. If Humphreys' success, then, in refusing to appear before the Senate committee is inexplicable, it did have the consequence of persuading Robert Kennedy to unleash hundreds of phone- and wire-tapping agents in pursuit of the Camel's colleagues. This decision was to embarrass him later when the Director of the FBI, J. Edgar Hoover, let it be known that he had done nothing which Kennedy had not approved of, knowledge the Kennedys' liberal friends did not care for.

Robert Kennedy's rage against the Outfit, both when he was chief counsel and, after January 1961, when he was attorney general in his brother's administration, is a rare and admirable flourish in American life. The question is whether he was so determined *because* his father had been a gangster before his wealth carried him as Ambassador to the Court of St James in London, supposing that the son knew of his father's history in the bootlegging battles of the twenties in Chicago. It is not given to many families in the Western world for one son to be a president, another an attorney general, intent on jailing a hood like Humphreys who had once sat down, so help us, with their own Dad in a room in Chicago and carved up the distribution of liquor in a state once they had stopped throwing bombs at one another. Was there, in his determination, some anguish about his parenthood? A desire to expunge the past, a bizarre form of patricide? The matter becomes more complicated if he was aware of his father's long affair with a Hollywood film star. Would that, in turn, explain his with Marilyn Monroe? Again, would it all become more complicated for him to discover that his brother, the president, had taken a girlfriend – arranged by the ubiquitous Humphreys – who had been the lady of the horrible Sam Giancanna – to wit, Judith Campbell Exner? It is not surprising that Robert Kennedy seemed like a man possessed. It may be, as some Americans argue, that

Bobby Kennedy was merely carrying out his father's orders: put my old enemies in jail, son.

The question therefore arises: why should Humphreys have had the Outfit support Senator John F. Kennedy's campaign for the presidency when his brother Robert was so determined to destroy them? Humphreys often expressed privately his dislike of Joe Kennedy, believing him to be an egomaniac. He thought the patriarch had done both John F. and Robert F. harm by seeking to express that mania through their careers. According to his daughter, Humphreys' view of the relationship between parents and children was that it should be an affectionate one in which the parent gently guided and taught the child. He thought Joe Kennedy terrorised his children into ambition and a passion for fame and money and power. Ergo: the children were weak, 'wimps'. That, of course, a gangster celebrated in the rackets, famous among murderers, the very image of a corrupter, should be so accustomed to speaking familiarly in his after-dinner chat of the rulers of the world's most powerful nation, has long ceased to surprise.

The reasons why the Outfit supported John F. Kennedy are to do with an idiocy about Cuba and common sense about Chicago; the idiocy was Giancanna's, the sense Humphreys'. Fidel Castro's triumph in Havana had caused general distress among the criminal classes in the United States. It was not merely that the senior gangsters enjoyed fishing in the Cuban waters: they owned the brothels and the gambling dens. Suddenly they had been deprived of pleasure and income. What was the government going to do about this grave interference with property and freedom? Surely a God-fearing Washington would reclaim the territory, restore the dictator Batista, the old pal, and have the girls and the gambling-wheels turning again. Sam Giancanna, always active in Cuba and Central America, seems to have been persuaded by wild elements in the CIA that he could play an heroic role in saving his investments by his exertions and the nation by his example. A Kennedy in office, son of friend Humphreys' old sparring partner Joe, would be the very man. Friend Humphreys was more sceptical, perhaps not seeing himself as a foreign affairs specialist. Giancanna was for invading Cuba and killing Castro. Humphreys was more troubled by a problem in Chicago, in the First Ward, that Loop which never ended.

There had been a fresh police scandal in Chicago. The Democratic boss, Mayor Richard J. Daley, had barely survived in power in 1959 when the citizens had discovered that practically all his police officers were on the take. The presidential election was in November 1960. Mayor Daley had already abandoned the local man, Adlai Stevenson, who was anxious to be the Democratic candidate for the third time. He had supported a fellow Irish Catholic John F. Kennedy and swung Illinois behind him. As Mike Royko devastatingly argues, though, in his biography of Daley – *The Boss* – the Chicago mayor regarded the election of Kennedy as secondary to the local battle. The machine, that engine invented, re-invented, refined and refuelled over the decades by Hinky Dink, the Bath, Kelly and Nash, with Humphreys so often courteously in attendance, now presided over by Daley, was to have a glorious hour. American commentators had already begun to suggest that radio and television had put an end to the capacity of the Outfit or the precinct, even, to deliver. The public would now be swayed by the image and not by the worker on the ground beguiling by the old devices. But Chicago was not yet done. Humphreys went to work.

Mike Royko, who was later, in his obituary of the Camel (see Chapter 16), to write one of the classic columns in American journalism, considers that the crisis for the machine, the Outfit and all who lived by these powerful engines of corruption and fortune, was represented by Benjamin Adamowski. This lawyer was the elected district attorney of Illinois State. He was a nuisance. He had revealed that when burglaries took place in Chicago, the burglars were often the police. Accustomed as the citizens were to fraudulence among the cops when it came to traffic offences or the behaviour of the courts, there did seem something, somehow, wrong about the police being burglars. Hard to put a finger on quite what was wrong, but it seemed not altogether right. Mayor Daley and the Camel saw the matter differently. The offence was the behaviour of Attorney Benjamin Adamowski. He had to be defeated in the November elections or who knows what else he might discover. Adamowski was standing as a Republican on the same ticket as Richard Nixon. John F. Kennedy (Democrat) was on the Daley ticket.

'Daley has stolen the White House,' said Adamowski when he learned that he had lost and that Kennedy had carried Illinois by ten thousand votes. These few votes enabled Kennedy to win enough Electoral College votes to make him president. Had they gone the other way Richard Nixon would have been elected and Camelot would not have come to the White House. All that romance and glamour would never have been. The Vietnam War might never have been. The Kennedy brothers might never have been assassinated.

After the Kennedy victory and before the new president welcomed Mayor Daley to the White House – 'We were the first family invited to the White House,' proclaimed the mayor, and why not? – there was uproar in Chicago. Mike Royko described the course of events once the Republicans and Adamowski had objected to the conduct of the poll:

Daley's election board soberly announced that it would be glad to conduct a recheck, and it began, one precinct a day. At that pace they would complete the recheck in twenty years. When they stopped stalling, it became obvious that if they hadn't stolen the White House or, more likely, Adamowski's office, it wasn't because they hadn't tried. In 900 precincts in which ballot papers were still used, the recheck caused a switch of ten thousand votes . . . Daley's election board members looked innocent throughout the limited recheck and blamed it all on human error, brought on by the fatigue of a long day and evening in the polling place. They didn't explain why the human errors consistently benefited Democrats.

The fraud was so obvious that Daley had to permit a special prosecutor to be appointed to investigate. More than six hundred polling-place workers and precinct captains were brought to trial. To assure that the fix would not be put in by a local judge, a downstate judge was called in to hear the cases. The downstate judge turned out to be a faithful organisation Democrat, and later most of the charges were wiped out.

The Kennedys, being a Boston-Irish family with an entertaining pedigree in that city's politics, would probably not have been surprised at the customary Chicago behaviour. To win by one vote is as fine a thing in a democracy as winning by millions and if that voter had been dead a long time, or was a horse: well, it had happened the other way around in Chicago from time to time. The distinction between Boston or New York and Chicago was that in the Windy City there was that dreadful tradition of the vote often carrying a bullet along with it, that murderous element which gave a politician, like the gangster, a sense that he was living on the dangerous edge of things. In that intoxicating time of John F. Kennedy's inauguration as president in January 1961 when he seemed to offer a youthful hope in his rhetoric to a troubled world, it would not have been convincing to suggest that he had won by votes fixed by a few unsalubrious elements in the Loop.

Bobby Kennedy was not inhibited. Now attorney general, he renewed his attack on the Outfit, the Mafia and the corrupt within government. In his three years in office, reports William V. Shannon in his portrait (*The Heir Apparent*), he prosecuted

> numerous Democratic politicians including two Congressmen, three State Supreme justices, five mayors, two chiefs of police, and three sheriffs. One of those convicted was New York State Supreme Court Justice Vincent Keogh, the brother of Congressman Eugene Keogh, an Administration stalwart on the House Ways and Means Committee and a personal intimate of President Kennedy.

His father used to say that 'Bobby hates like I do.' His fervour for justice, however complicated his motive, was to have its effect. The mobsters would not, in the nature of things, step on to a public platform to denounce the new president and his brother, but their associates certainly would when they could. Jimmy Hoffa took the opportunity of his annual Teamsters' Union conference at Miami Beach, Florida early in July 1961 to let the attorney general know his view.

Murray Humphreys had called in at the conference since he happened to be staying at his mansion nearby, using the name Lewis Hart – or was it Harris? He heard the two thousand Teamster delegates cheer his friend Jimmy Hoffa 'wildly', as reports had it, and must have taken pleasure in seeing how well he had done – that young man he had nurtured in the ways of trade union and commercial life so long ago. Attorney General Kennedy had already lost two cases in prosecuting Hoffa for corruption. The London *Economist* reported:

> Few trade union gatherings have received as much attention as the one that the teamsters have just concluded in Miami Beach, Florida. According to Mr Hoffa, the watchers included the government forces which are still actively pursuing him. Before the convention he charged that more than 150 agents of the Federal Bureau of Investigation were scouring the country looking for any signs of illegality in the choice of delegates or anything else that might be used to prevent him from being confirmed in the presidency, to which he thought he was more than entitled. During the convention Mr Hoffa warned the delegates that female agents of the government might use their wiles to uncover evidence against him; and later during the proceedings he showed the delegates an electronic listening device which he said had been hidden in a television set to eavesdrop on his conversations.

Later Hoffa was to go to jail briefly and then to be murdered in unexplained circumstances, but this day he was expressing not only the feelings of the meeting but those of the observing Camel. The Kennedy 'buggings' were beginning to be a problem, along with the computer the attorney general had introduced into the Justice Department. Murray Humphreys, now in his sixties and by his daughter's account longing to give up his profession and having suffered a mild heart attack, had been presented with one of his most taxing tasks – and by a president he had helped to elect. That his genius, that ever-sparkling spring of invention, was not exhausted he was soon to demonstrate. In the meantime there was the question of Cuba and Giancanna. The life of the prince is not an easy one, the demands on his energy and guile being ceaseless, especially when his company takes the view that a gun can settle every problem.

Giancanna saw the disastrous Bay of Pigs enterprise – in which a motley mob hastily assembled by the CIA, with or without the president's support, attempted to re-take Cuba, only to founder in the water – as a serious effort by the Kennedys to repay their debt to the Outfit which had supported their election to power. Since Giancanna had been engaged in covert conversation with the CIA to kill Castro he could not be blamed at detecting a connection between his aspirations and those of the president. It may be that his analysis was correct. Or it may have been, given the tense hours that subsequently troubled the world when President Kennedy and Mr Khrushchev confronted each other about the Soviet presence in Cuba, that the US government had preoccupations other than the fate of the mob's brothels and gambling houses in Havana. Giancanna's opinion was that the Kennedys had let him down.

The brooding Camel removed himself from these grand questions of state. How was he to prevent the damaging inroads the attorney general was making on his colleagues and their political and judicial friends? As ever, he addressed himself to the important question. What exactly was the attorney general doing? He was intruding on the private conversations of citizens of the United States, free men whose rights were protected by a venerable constitution. Was this not a monstrous interference with the liberty of the subject? Why should he, Llewelyn Morris Humphreys, when meeting colleagues at Schneiders or at the Armoury for a meal or drink, or at the Desert Inn in Nevada, have his private chat overheard? Therefore Attorney General Kennedy, a member of a family synonymous with liberal thinking, his president brother the darling of the high-minded intelligentsia, was an enemy of the rights of the citizen. Something had to be done. Particularly it had to be done because Anthony Accardo was in jail and a little cross that the Camel hadn't shown his usual skill in keeping him out of so unpleasant and unlikely a place. (The Humphreys view was that he could scarcely be held responsible for friends going to jail on income tax charges: his responsibility was for more serious matters.) Scores of other colleagues were becoming troubled by FBI agents tailing them, surrounding their houses, plaguing their girlfriends, upsetting their travels.

The Camel approached his old friend Congressman Roland V. Libonati, a man on whose piano he'd laid his gun on that famous night in the wild old days when Libonati had been elected to the Illinois State Assembly; the man who had defended him in the even more famous Double Jeopardy trial in 1939. Also, of course, the man the FBI had observed accepting from the Camel a parcel thought to contain green-backs at the Woodner Hotel in Washington in May 1960, not to mention the same Libonati with whom Humphreys had discussed the parole of Paul Ricca from the penitentiary at Terre Haute. In other words; the faithful 'Libby' Libonati. He was in Washington now and an important man. More, was he not part of the Chicago machine which had brought President Kennedy to his narrow victory and along with him many trucks on the gravy train?

It is difficult for those who are not American politicians or gangsters to guess at quite how the conversation went. From what I have heard of Humphreys' tone in his films and from the accounts of his style from those who knew him, it is feasible that he opened his speech, or orders, to the congress-man with general remarks on the importance of the liberty of the citizen. He may have continued by saying that life was becoming very difficult. Probably he would have told the congressman than some members of the relevant House Judiciary Committee had certain weaknesses, were perhaps beholden in this way or that, perhaps needed cash for their re-election, or whatever. And wouldn't there, anyway, be plenty of enemies of the Kennedys on the committee?

Libonati went to work on his campaign to have a motion accepted by the Democratic majority to 'investigate the Justice Department's activities concerning individual rights and liberties as guaranteed by the Constitution and the laws

143

of the United States regardless of the administration in power'. The attorney general, furious, warned the Chicago machine that he found Libonati's cheek so intolerable that if their man were to stay in the Congress after the next election he would have him arrested. Libonati agreed not to stand again but the resolution was passed by the attorney general's own party. Before the matter could be pursued any further Robert Kennedy was no longer in office: his brother, the president, had been murdered in Dallas.

American presidents had been assassinated before and an attempt has been made since on President Reagan, but in each case except that of John F. Kennedy it has been reasonable to regard the dreadful fact as the aberration of a self-willed killer. The death of President Kennedy is bewildering. His murder in Dallas is one of the shocking events of the late twentieth century. He was, in his time, the very image of a statesman. That, subsequently, the image may not have been the true man is irrelevant: a politician who can manage to be so for his people and epoch has done enough. His death was seen as a tragedy, the cruel end of a bold, handsome hope. Seen, though, from the perspective of the Outfit his murder is less surprising. The assumption is general in Chicago that he was killed by agents either of the Syndicate or the Mafia, more probably the former since the Mafia is not held in high regard. In a not altogether mysterious manner, the Kennedys were regarded by the Outfit as a presidential family that belonged. Belonged to precisely what is not so clear. Probably to immigrants, associated through Joe Kennedy's bootlegging and Hollywood days with the wild, successful Irish. Therefore there was at best a disappointment, at worst a betrayal, at the failure over Cuba and the even more distressing puritanism of Robert Kennedy. This is probably to grace the attitude of the hoodlums. Brutally, if they shot him it is because that is their simple solution to every problem.

There is no evidence that the Camel had any hand in the murder of the president or its arrangement. He seems to have shared the general view that the Kennedys were bound to meet trouble at the hands of the Outfit. The Camel's own concern in his last years was to resume his family life with his first wife and with his daughter. He made little effort to keep the obnoxious Giancanna out of jail early in 1965. He reflected, as survivors will, on what chance it had been that so few of the great and the bad he had worked with were still alive, that he had escaped the bullet, the pineapple, even jail. He had not long to live but in his last months he was still to demonstrate to his loyal Chicago public that he had a trick and some wit to offer.

15   Humphreys dies: heart attack blamed

HIS EPITAPH: NO GANGSTER WAS MORE BOLD
Headline, *Chicago Sun-Times*, November 1965

Humphreys died of unnatural causes – a heart attack.
Mike Royko

When I heard that he was dead it was like a friend of the family or a relative had passed away. A chapter in my life was ending. I didn't sleep hardly at all that night. I knew that he was a murderer, an extortionist and an acid thrower and everything. I knew all the bad things. But in the fifty or so contacts that I had with Murray Humphreys, I learned to have a grudging respect for that man and I knew I was never going to see him again and that saddened me.
William Roemer, FBI agent, in conversation, 1983

Q: 'Do you have any comment on your arrest, Mr Humphreys?'
A: 'My, but you are a very pretty girl.'
Humphreys' last words: to a television interviewer, 23 November 1965

The explanations of Murray Humphreys' decision in June 1965 to visit his daughter and first wife at the ranch in Oklahoma rather than appear before the grand jury in Chicago are contradictory and each in turn contains its contradictions. The family view is firm. He had innocently come to see them. There were a few domestic business affairs

146

to be discussed. He was his usual cheerful self, reconciled to the fact that the state of his heart was not good and that he could have another attack at any time. Four years later the Chicago columnist Art Petaque was to publish a speculation which had haunted the mob after the Camel's death – although he was more than ever known as Curly in his last years because of his fine head of white hair – about the whereabouts of his great fortune. There was supposed to be some $10 million in cash somewhere. His daughter has told me that he certainly did not mention it on this visit, the last time she was to see her father alive.

He appeared to be delighted to be in the house that he had built himself and quite untroubled both by his fresh income tax trouble over the First National Life Insurance Company stock deal and by the jailing of Sam Giancanna. The family were aware of how much difficulty Giancanna had created. They aver that as soon as he heard on the radio that a warrant had been served on him in Chicago – news confirmed when brother Ernest phoned – he left to catch a train from Norman station nearby to accept the subpoena sworn at William Roemer's request; that he decided to take the train rather than use his return air ticket from Oklahoma City to Chicago since he had calculated he would be there sooner. Humphreys himself argued that he had left the telephone number of his lawyer with the FBI – he never answered his own telephone – so that he could be reached any time he was wanted. It was by chance that he gave the wrong number and had offered, instead of his lawyer's, the number of a construction company in Chicago: it was scarcely his fault if that office chose to deny knowledge of him. Moreover, would he have bought himself a return air ticket if he wasn't aiming to return?

William Roemer took – and takes still – a different view. He says that he had good reason to think that Humphreys really was going to stay away from Chicago. The prosecution device whereby Giancanna was imprisoned presented Humphreys with an equal difficulty. While infinitely cleverer than the hood he had come to despise, and perhaps because so perceptive, he recognised the trap this time of retreating to that haven of pleading the Fifth Amendment which he had

147

invented so long ago. Perhaps the jig really was up. By this FBI reading Humphreys had gone to the Norman railway station rather than use his return air ticket to Chicago not in the interests of speed but rather to rehearse a fresh disguise and leave the country. Wouldn't that provide a motive for a visit to the family, to his old house and hunting and bird-watching ground? Perhaps he had in mind to retire to Wales? Therefore, the FBI had been fortunate to catch him just in time and arrest him at Norman station. Humphreys was shocked at this analysis and furious that he was handcuffed when arrested, like some kind of criminal.

Whatever the truth, when Humphreys appeared in court in his home city he was, to judge from the newspaper reports, in commanding form. His opening gambit was to have his lawyer Maurice J. Walsh suggest that the jury was illegal on the ground that the clerk of the federal court had not called out the names of the jurors as they were drawn. US District Attorney Hanrahan protested that all this was 'an abuse of the court's process'. Humphreys next offered a petition to quash the subpoena under which he had been ordered to appear. The infuriated Judge Campbell told the Camel that: 'The grand jury does not have to explain to you why it is going into anything. They are doing what I hope you will do – their duty as citizens of the United States. You are not to argue with them.' At which point a woman member of the jury asked Humphreys: 'Are you proud, would you be proud, to be an American citizen?' To which he replied that he refused to answer on the ground that it might tend to incriminate him.

Since Humphreys had been made to place a bond for the huge sum of $100,000 to enable him to be free to live at his opulent flat in the skyscraper Marina Building across the Chicago River from the court, the public, or such as had failed to escape the August heat, grew convinced that the 'brainy hood' was on the same route to jail as the thug Giancanna. The detail of his questioning had a traditional air about it. Would the Camel care to explain the significance of a party held with a few surviving Capone colleagues on the anniversary in 1962 of the St Valentine Day Massacre? Why did he see so much of the Democratic Party's First Ward boss

Pat Marcy? He had nothing to say. Only at one point did Humphrey lose his temper. He was asked if a trip he had made to France in 1963 had anything to do with narcotics? He replied at length, saying he had nothing to do with narcotics and never had. Everyone knew that about him. He did not add that he had been on a European trip, taking in Wales, in the company of both his first and second wives, no doubt judging that to be no one's business. What he did add was that if he was going to be asked any more questions about narcotics he doubted if he would return to talk to the grand jury.

Mostly, though, Humphreys beamed at the court as he had that day twenty-six years earlier when the case against him in the McLane Affair collapsed and for much the same reason. He had his attorney, Maurice Walsh, ask the judge whether the object of this appearance was to follow the precedent set by Giancanna's, whereby it was 'an attempt to create a situation for the offence of contempt and have him incarcerated'. Judge William Campbell called US Attorney Edward Hanrahan before the bench and asked him if such was the government's intention. 'Hanrahan replied: "No, it is not my present intention."' And so the $100,000 bond was cancelled without the prosecution putting up a fight, the grand jury was stood down and Humphreys strolled away. Could it really be magic? All done by mirrors?

This unexpected development – although given the Camel's history it should not have surprised the FBI as much as it did – might suggest that the Humphreys version of the flight into Oklahoma was correct. What did he have to fear from the grand jury? He must have known in June that he would not, in August, meet Sam Giancanna's fate and finish up in jail. After all, he and the rest of the Outfit hierarchy were as fed up with Giancanna as was the government. The grand jury would surely believe his account, too, of his trip to his family as, indeed, it appeared to. Surely even the maestro of corruption, the incomparable manipulator of public officials, couldn't have managed such a 'fix' in just five weeks? Assurances must have been given earlier. Whichever was the case the indefatigable FBI agent Roemer, even if baffled by this latest instance of Chicago's cultural

149

peculiarities, remained determined. The children in the parks might still, after the most recent city police scandals, play the new game of 'cops and cops': the Feds were different.

On 23 November 1965 William Roemer decided that he had enough evidence to swear out a warrant for the arrest of the sixty-six-year-old statesman of the Outfit. He described to me the events of the day and their consequences:

I had developed certain evidence after the grand jury hearing that I knew would prove that Murray Humphreys committed perjury that day. He had been asked if he knew or did not know when he went to Oklahoma that a subpoena had been served on him. He said he did not. I knew that he did know. So he was not speaking the truth to the grand jury. So the FBI took out a warrant for his arrest for perjury.

I did not want to be the guy that arrested Murray Humphreys. I had met him so many times that I had a certain regard for him. I didn't want to be there in the moment of his acute embarrassment. So we sent three of our very best agents, most capable, most experienced men, up to Humphreys' apartment on the fifty-first floor of the Marina Building, to arrest him. They announced themselves, shouted very loudly that they were FBI agents and that they had a warrant for his arrest. He refused to open the door. So they announced that they would kick the door down, that they were coming through that door whatever happened. At that point he opened the door and confronted them with a pistol. They could have shot him right there. They had every legal right to do so: they had a warrant for his arrest, he pulled a pistol on them. But they didn't, they refrained, and I think the reason they refrained was because it was Murray Humphreys. If it had been Sam Giancanna they would probably have been very quick to dispatch him. These agents didn't know Humphreys personally but they knew his image, so they didn't kill him. They wrestled with him and took his gun and went into the apartment which they had every right to do and said they were going to conduct a search incidental to the arrest.

Humphreys felt that the FBI agents had to have a search warrant, that the arrest warrant wasn't sufficient in itself. He fought with them. We knew that he had a safe in that apartment and that in the safe he had a black book and in that black book were the names of all the people he had corrupted, all the public officials, all the judges, all the law-enforcement officers; and their telephone numbers and addresses. We wanted that black book. He, for the same reasons that we wanted it, didn't want us to have it. He had the keys to the safe in his pocket. He put his hand in his pocket. He refused to let the agents have the keys so that they had to rip the pocket off forcibly. It was an emotional situation and a very distressing one for Humphreys. The FBI agents brought him down town and he was arraigned and let out on bail of $100,000. Later that evening I saw him on television where he was as witty and charming as ever. Later that evening I had a phone call and heard that he was dead, of a heart attack, in his apartment.

The body was discovered at 8.30 p.m. by his ever-faithful elder brother Ernest who was still helping in the business. The family came up from Oklahoma, his first wife Mary, daughter Llewella, and her young son George. Humphreys had not wanted any but the family at his funeral, none of the Outfit or its satraps, and so it was, except that they did allow the FBI agent Roemer, of whom he had seen so much, to come to pay his last respects.

The Chicago papers had cleared the front pages to carry the news of the death of one of its sons who, for all his efforts to avoid the light, manifestly figured in the files of the *Tribune, News* and *Sun-Times* more prominently than he could have wanted. The news stories had an heroic ring: 'Humphreys Picked Up Capone's Mantle' the *Daily News* had it, observing:

Although Humphreys started out as a pistol-packing ruffian, he soon found that his brains spoke louder than his muscle. Those who met the handsome, soft-spoken, seemingly so well-mannered man of recent years found it hard to believe that he once was identified as one of the gunmen

151

who shot down seven rival gangsters in the 1929 killing
that is still known the world over as the St Valentine's Day
Massacre . . . At the time of his death Humphreys was still
the crime syndicate's master fixer, the man who could
'reach out for' a judge, a policeman or even a Congressman.

As the news pages offered thousands of words on the
Camel's exploits from his days as a child prodigy of crime,
the editorials showed a higher sense of duty. DEATH OF A
'SMART' HOODLUM was the *Daily News* heading:

As thugs go Murray Humphreys was smarter than most.
One proof of this is the fact that some 32 years after a
Chicago police official told him to get out of town because
his day was done, Humphreys was still in town and pre-
sumably still plying his shadowy trade . . . Like most
gangsters, Humphreys shielded his private life from view
which led to a lot of speculation about his activities and his
income . . . But it sounds as if the one-time successor to Al
Capone as Chicago's king pin gangster had made a rather
glamorous life for himself over the years . . . It is fitting to
wonder, though, how often through the years he had sat
too frightened to answer a knock on his door, and what he
would have given for an unconditional release from the
bondage of his fear.

The *Sun-Times* offered AFFLUENT GUNMAN:

Murray (The Camel) Humphreys whose first name was
really Llewelyn was a grammar school drop-out before
World War 1. Like many others of his generation he
became a self-educated success in his field. While other
men started at the bottom as messengers and clerks and
worked their way up to become executives of business,
Humphreys started at the bottom of his field as a
burglar and hired gunman and worked to the top in the
Crime Syndicate.
On the way Humphreys became a protégé of Al
Capone, an associate of some public officials whose sense

of ethics was no higher than his own and he learned to speak drawing room English like an Eliza Doolittle of the underworld. He was a product of our times, of the age of prohibition and the later period of labour racketeering. Although he often moved in respectable circles in his Florida home, virtually he remained a criminal at war with society. Humphreys, like Capone, could exert power and live lavishly only in a society that tolerated him.

In Chicago it was not curious, this publishing of grave leading articles about a gangster. It is not easy to think of such appearing in *The Times* of London, *Le Monde*, or *Süddeutsche Zeitung*. Easier to understand in the case of *Corriere della Sera* on the death of Signor Calvi, the activities of the P2 freemasons' lodge, the Bank Ambrosiano and its Chicago Archbishop Marcinkus. The obituaries do not touch on important aspects of Humphreys' later career and especially his role in big business, in laundering money for corporations. The secret, perhaps, had been too well kept? Or was it a matter best left alone?

A week after the Camel's death the *Daily News* returned to his career in a column by its famous wit, Mike Royko. He wrote:

It wouldn't be right to let Murray Humphreys pass from the scene without mentioning one of his lesser-known but important functions in local affairs. Humphreys was a highly skilled talent scout. According to scholars of such matters, he was the crime syndicates' leading recruiter of young blood, if you'll pardon the expression. He could reach into the backwoods and find a talented machine-gun player in much the same way that George Halas [the football coach] sometimes spots star material in little colleges . . . Many of the men who developed into outstanding figures owed a debt to their discoverer Humphreys. If the subject of retiring the Camel ever came up, someone surely blubbered, 'Gee, but it was Murray who gave me my first break. I was just a nothing – then he let me shoot somebody.'

The list of people he discovered, cultivated, taught and

helped boost to success reads like an all-star team of undesirables. Humphreys could boast and probably did, that nobody he ever brought in turned out to be less than a complete slob. In Jasper, Alabama, of all places he found the fabled Sam (Golf Bag) Hunt. There was Sam probably running around Jasper barefoot looking for a turnip to steal when Humphreys spotted him. He brought Hunt to Chicago and gave him a machine gun and assigned him to the job of keeping people from harming their leader Al Capone. Sam Giancanna was little more than an unknown semi-illiterate when Humphreys took him in hand. Today Giancanna is a well-known semi-illiterate. His big break came when Humphreys assigned him to a team of messengers, errand boys, drivers and bodyguards for the wives of Ricca, Campagna and Gioe who were in federal prison at the time. It was Humphreys who promoted Hyman Gottfried to the role of a courier. He could read a little which helped him find street addresses.

James (Cat Eyes) Catura had no real direction in life until Humphreys put him to work blowing up people and things. During the thirties when he was helping the syndicate get into organised labour, he brought along many non-labouring labour leaders such as Joey Glimco, who kept his foot on the throats of Chicago's labour leaders for many years while leading them.

Nobody knows how Humphreys did it. Some people thought that he would rap a prospect on the head and if he heard a bongo drum sound, he knew he had a recruit. Others said that Humphreys would judge a prospect by his parents. If he had any, he was discarded. There is another theory that his system was no more complicated than turning over a rock and seeing what crawled out.

Mr Royko's severe judgment was balanced by another appraisal in which the Welshman 'devised legal strategies and political fixes that have yet to be equalled. He engendered appreciation for his immense intellect, his finesse and, again within the perspective of his vocation, his civility.'

However mixed the panegyrics and however modest his funeral – itself symbolic of his thesis that the mob had to change its ways and follow his quiet example – those colleagues, and the public officials, whether in the law or politics, who had been awed by him in life were to be beguiled by him, too, in death. ARE CRYPTIC FIGURES THE KEY TO CAMEL'S 10 MILLION DOLLAR CACHE? was the headline on an Art Petaque article in the March 1969 *Chicago Sun-Times*. 'Investigators,' he writes,

> have tracked down hundreds of leads and the notation 'No 46-400 at 20' still stumps them. It turned up on one of the 17 pages of loose-leaf notes found in Humphreys' 51st floor Marina City apartment by federal agents who arrested the gangster. Could it be a code to the location? . . . An indication of his income can be gauged from the tax case the government prepared against him for the years 1957 to 1962. His known income was $452,111. How much he was able to hide from the government can only be guessed. Immense profits flowed to him from the mob's gambling enterprises. Humphreys reportedly owned a piece of the action at two of the biggest casinos in Las Vegas, Nevada, before he died . . . Communiqués to Swiss banks and checks with US banks on holders of safe-deposit boxes have failed to turn up a hoard.

And in 1984, Mr Petaque told me, the money had still not been found. When I asked his daughter about it, she laughed: perhaps it had been 'Mr Moneybags's' last witticism, perpetuating mischief into the posthumous.

If the favourable death notices had about them something of the elegance of Winston Churchill's elegy on the death of his friend, David Lloyd George – 'His swift, penetrating, comprehensive mind was always grasping at the root of any question. His eye ranged ahead of the obvious. He was always hunting in the fields beyond' – none raised the question of whether it was necessary for Llewelyn Morris Humphreys to be a gangster. Was it inevitable, some dark force in his nature, or was it mere social and cultural chance that he spent his life in the Outfit? When raised, the question produced responses as mixed as the obituaries.

His daughter Llewella recalls her father saying of the

Outfit, once the 'shoot-em-up' Prohibition days were over, that it killed fewer people than supposedly respectable firms did in the normal course of business. And even in the bootlegging days the murders were between, or within, the gangs. But she argues that it is important to remember the period in which he grew up. At the age of seven he was

on a street corner selling newspapers for a living. And in Chicago to make the most money you had to have the best corner and you had to get up very early and fight to see who could win the best corner. A bloody nose was not uncommon. He tended to be a bit of a fighter, hot tempered. My mother told me that once a week she would have to go and fetch him out of jail for fighting. But the truth is that he very often said that he regretted his profession, but that he had made his decision and he had to stick with it. In his young days you either were educated or you went into the Organisation. There were no other ways of making money and he vowed that his family would never do without in the way he had done without. I remember one night when I was in high school I heard him – he and mother were talking, thinking I was asleep – and he said: 'I'm so tired, I want out so bad, but I can't, I have to live with it.' That must have been about 1950 and it became worse when the bugging started. The privacy that he had always tried to arrange no longer existed.

FBI agent William Roemer for all his high regard for Humphreys, or perhaps because of it, would not accept the daughter's appraisal.

A lot of people grew up in the same neighbourhood in the same era and they didn't turn out to be gangsters and mobsters. I feel just the opposite argument applies to Murray Humphreys. He had a talent and a native intelligence that would have enabled him to do anything. He could have been a success in any aspect of our society. It was a shame that he associated with these animals – because that is what they are – the dregs of society. His working on their behalf enabled them to be so much more effective and efficient than they would ever have been if it hadn't been for Murray Humphreys.

Mr Irwin Weiner, however, who was the bondsman who put up the $100,000 bail for Murray Humphreys in the last months of his life, could see no reason why the Welshman should have done other than he did. His admiration for the Camel's courage, elegance, generosity and talents is complete, his memory still warm. The day I met Mr Weiner in the Loop in 1983 he was irritated that the Chicago Crime Commission had included his name in a list of members of the Outfit, which he thought unfair; and he was still shaken by having the Teamsters' Union leader Allen Dorfman recently shot dead alongside him in a hotel car park in the city. He would not accept the argument that the great gangster could have been a fine political leader: 'Murray was too truthful, so I don't know how good a politician he would have been since one of the prime requisites of being a politician is not to be truthful.'

His tomb stands on a mound in a copse in the long grass of the parkland surrounding the house he built in Oklahoma. His surname alone is carved in the marble: no Christian names. In life the prince saw no reason to attract attention to himself, similarly in death.

16   The Camel's inheritance

Men rage against Materialism, as they call it, forgetting
that there has been no material improvement that has not
spiritualised the world, and that there have been few, if
any, spiritual awakenings that have not wasted the world's
faculties in barren hopes, and fruitless aspirations, and
empty or trammelling creeds. What is termed Sin is an
essential element of progress. Without it the world would
stagnate, or grow old, or become colourless. By its curiosity Sin increases the experience of the race. Through its
intensified assertion of individualism, it saves us from the
monotony of type. In its rejection of the current notions
about morality, it is one with the higher ethics.

Oscar Wilde

> The hand that signed the paper felled a city;
> Five sovereign fingers taxed the breath,
> Doubled the globe of dead and halved a country;
> These five kings did a king to death . . .

Dylan Thomas
Twenty-Five Poems, 1936

Just as every migrant group in the United States, whether
of European, South American or Asian origin, will feel the
nation belongs to them, so most foreigners have their own
America in the mind. Any judgment of Llewelyn Morris
Humphreys' career and achievement will be coloured by the
pallet it is painted on. Fugitive and cloistered minds will
regard him as yet another demonstration that the United
States, bearing the banner of capitalism, is as corrupt as the
Soviet Union in the communist corner, the one through the

ruthless ambition for cash, the other for an equally debilitating spiritual pursuit of power. Such extremism is not helpful in gauging the insidiousness of Humphreys' insights and capacity.

Knowing about Murray Humphreys demonstrates how the melodramatic representation of the Mafia in *The Godfather* distracted attention from a more serious corruption. Why should it not still be doing so? When the mob or Outfit or Syndicate are presented as being gaudy and easily recognised members of a particular race, the members can be isolated as an apparent aberration in a society. Identify a Capone or any of his less celebrated successors and you have a dangerous yet comfortable idea: these are hoodlums beyond the pale. Concentrate on their peculiar loyalties and savage customs, persuade yourself that they kill within the circles of their sodality, and the respectable world, if not altogether safe from the stray bullet, is formally inviolate. To say of that man sitting across the bar or the restaurant that he is a member of the Outfit, as one might say he's a famous actor or writer, is more agreeable than having to wonder if the lawyer or businessman or politician who is in your company derives his income from a more mysterious manifestation of that same mob.

Given that Humphreys was at all successful in seeing to it that gangster funds went into respectable commercial enterprises – and his talent at everything else he turned his hand to would suggest so – any sentient man in American commercial life is in an odd position. Either he doesn't know if the Outfit's money supports his enterprise, and worries; or he does know, and worries: not every businessman, of course, is sentient, so that many may consider the matter a nonsense. It's common gossip in most of the world's financial centres, London as much as Tokyo, that Mafia money is coming into town: who fancies it? The prospect is more taxing when it is Mafia money arriving without anyone knowing that it is such, but travelling incognito, as Humphreys was wont to.

In the past in America bold spirits have shared Oscar Wilde's opinion that without Sin the 'world would stagnate, or grow old, or become colourless', have agreed with him that it intensifies individualism. Wilde may have been frivolous; those who adored the buccaneering antics of the robber barons, the Fisks and Goulds, the Rockefellers and Vanderbilts, J. P. Morgan and Carnegie, the skulduggery of Insull and Yerkes, the flamboyance of Colosimo and Capone, of Hinky Dink and the Bath, were being serious. This was the vigour of the New World, creating and stealing wealth, the stuff of a wild, new society where everything goes. Sin it may be and, true, many suffer but, kid, it's fun. This cheerful rejoicing in wickedness is no longer heard.

Even if more blandly, even incomprehensibly, expressed in the new Germanised American language, that drive of the robber barons remains the society's main engine. If Wilde is right, material improvement has been spiritualised in the United States. That passion to make money, the desire to win, is assumed to be a necessary condition of a democratic society. No recent piece of Americana has been more revealing, if awful, than the presentation of the 1984 Olympic Games in Los Angeles. 'Going for Gold' was the slogan, Mammon apotheosised across the night skies of California. Not going out for pleasure, or comradeship, or skill: gold. That most people who have ever played games have a pretty low view of team-mates or rivals to whom winning is everything was not accommodated in the US slogan. If one is to judge a society by such sports players, terms like insecure, troubled, a sense of inadequacy, a feeling of being unloved, would be the first to come to mind.

Let's suppose, then, that the worship of Mammon is the spiritual fuel in the American engine, that it really has come a long way from Pennsylvania, not to mention Virginia, from Thomas Jefferson and the Adams family, or Boston's grand families who spoke only to God; how much does it matter if such a society is corrupted? When Humphreys held his long sway, how much was the citizen troubled when, shall we say, he sat on a jury and heard the suave Welshman win an acquittal to the fury of the prosecution? Did the juryman know that the judge might have been bought; that the prosecuting lawyer was a stooge; the police fixed? If he did, or did not, how seriously did he reflect on the noble aspirations of his Constitution? When a manager in an insurance or construction company discovered that honest business could not be done because the Outfit had an arrangement with City

Hall, how disturbed was his faith in the nature of his democracy? These would be relatively tranquil disturbances contrasted with the violent intrusions of the mob's men at your place of work or your apartment or bar, but more troubling perhaps if you took your nation's pretensions solemnly.

Most of us in our own professions are aware of the debilitating effect of minor corruption, mostly taking the form of the fiddling of expenses or hours of work. When a conspiracy exists whereby it is generally known in an enterprise that the board of directors, managers, staff or workers, all are indulging what in Britain are known as 'Spanish practices', then it may seem, if illegal, an agreeable arrangement. What can be wrong, when everyone is doing it? Yet it seems to create, even among people who might boast about their tricks, a general unease, a shiftiness, as if some deep moral seam is being touched, indefinable, half-forgotten when discernible; and so the quality of work and enthusiasm for a skill is diminished. If that happens on so commonplace a level, what reason is there to suppose that the effect is different in a grander, more sonorous context?

Humphreys worked on the assumption that everyone had his price, and unfortunately never saw any reason among all the wide range of prominent fellow citizens he dealt with, ever to change his analysis. It could be that he was careful not to approach people who knew the value rather than the price of selling themselves, or is that a generous cavil? His cynicism is shared by many. That everyone is on the make is a general assumption, And yet there remains, as Lloyd George observed, that vague desire to aspire to something higher in the life of the whole society. President Nixon, after all, did fall from power even if his fall took a long time and is still thought by many of his fellows to be an unnecessarily harsh consequence of behaviour that was scarcely all that unusual. This surely demonstrates a public desire for proper behaviour. It also shows that Richard Nixon, one of the most experienced of American politicians, saw nothing wrong.

If corruption matters in a society it is because a democratic leadership needs to make demands on its people, like at worst conscripting them for war, which may be easy in a totalitarian state, but can be met with hostility or indifference if the people do not trust the leaders making the demands. The dreadful behaviour I watched of US conscripts in Vietnam was a brutal consequence. If this is a potential problem in a small society, how much more so in a huge federal empire where the character of the population changes endlessly? The wild effect of Chicago on an older American tradition was dramatic; the incursion of South Americans and Asians will further dilute the language of an old puritanism. If citizens grow sceptical about the legality of authority, and government wishes to preserve its power, its logic will be to become more authoritarian; not a pretty thought. The old rhetoric remains (Mammon and the going for gold not lending themselves to more than hucksterism and hype), but wears thinner.

The happy thought is that there cannot any more be a Humphreys in American life, that he was an historical accident, born perfectly in his time. No more will a man move easily among political leaders, judges, lawyers, trade union leaders and businessmen of all kinds, actors and singers and above all gangster colleagues, persuading all to his will, carrying in his pocket not only votes and money-bribes, but a threat of death. Yet there was once a belief that the sinister days of crime had ended with Capone, that it was an unfortunate consequence of Prohibition alone.

How can we be sure there is no Humphreys now? He evaded attention most of his lifetime. It is hard to believe that any successor would possess all his gifts and especially not the wry, laconic manner in which he held up a slightly distorted mirror to the formal goals of American society. Moneybags, the brainy Welsh hood, Curly, the Hump, the Camel was, as his fellow Chicagoans recognised, the 'boldest of them all', unique in his murderous community. However, there may be lesser men, achieving not so much but carrying forward the tradition he established of a fruitful relationship between law and crime, between the elected representatives of the people and the laundering of dishonest gain. Even without a successor, his inheritance would ensure that the 'disease' so cogently diagnosed by Machiavelli so long ago remained virulent enough to disturb any sanguine view of the world's most powerful nation.

162

Cast-list of characters

ACCARDO, Anthony Joseph.
A bodyguard for Al Capone and a suspect in the St Valentine Day Massacre, who was employed by Humphreys or rather paid a salary by Humphreys, in the brewery and laundry business. After Humphreys' death in 1965 Accardo, who had been arrested at least thirty times on charges as varied as murder, extortion and tax evasion, assumed control of the Outfit.

AIUPPA, Joseph.
A minor gangster in Humphreys' time, who became an important ally of Accardo when the Welshman died.

ALEX, Gus.
An important ally of Humphreys in the Loop, particularly in his work among politicians, trade union leaders, lawyers and gamblers. A familiar suspect in murder and bribery cases.

BIOFF, William.
In the late thirties the union leader, who under Humphreys' instruction corrupted Hollywood, but would not name the Welshman in evidence which sent Ricca, Nitti, Fischetti and Campagna to jail. Later Bioff was murdered.

CAMPAGNA, Louis.
An expert marksman. Brought in as an assassin by Capone; known as 'Little New York'. Humphreys was to use him after Capone's death to support whoever was needed at the head of the Outfit or the Mafia.

163

CAPONE, Alphonse.
Capone, the most famous of gangsters who depended on Humphreys' talent towards the end of the twenties; was also known as Scarface, Little Caesar or Big Al. While his political judgment was often poor his control of his own troops was complete. Mysteriously Humphreys seems to have done nothing to have Capone removed from prison, even though exercising ingenuity to bring about the parole of others. Probably the task was too much, although this failure did increase Humphreys' power.

CERMAK, Anton.
A Democratic politician in Chicago, who was assassinated while he was mayor in 1933, standing alongside the newly elected Democratic President, Franklin D. Roosevelt. He was elected mayor in the belief that he was an enemy of crime. This was a misapprehension. He had his own gang in mind. This was probably why he was shot, leading to a view that no one wanted to shoot the President; Cermak was the target.

COLOSIMO, James.
Known as Big Jim. He began his career as a street sweeper at the turn of the century. Married a brothel owner and grew rich in the white slave and gambling trades. His restaurant attracted Caruso, Galli-Curci, Tetrazzini and John McCormack. He probably set the tone for twentieth-century Chicago crime. He proves one point; an acolyte murdered him when Prohibition began: that tradition existed before bootlegging.

COUGHLIN, John.
Known as Bath House or the Bath. Coughlin exploited his proprietorship of the bath house he owned as a source of votes. His Irish Catholic connections established his power. He gave memorable parties. His influence diminished in the twenties when Capone pursued a more maverick policy and even abandoned the Bath's Democrats for the Republicans.

DARROW, Clarence.
One of the most eloquent of American lawyers whose heroic defence of radical trade union leaders in violent times at the turn of the century was followed by the defence of others who were gangsters of Humphreys' acquaintance.

De LUCIA, Paul.
Better known as Paul (The Waiter) Ricca. A great fan of Humphreys although a senior Mafia figure. He was always impressed by the Welshman's capacity to settle matters with the authorities.

DALEY, Richard.
Known as 'the Boss', he ensured in the fifties and sixties that the Democratic machine built up by Hinky Dink, the Bath, Cermak, Kelly and Nash kept control of the city and of Cook County, the territory of larger Chicago. He suffered from scandals but survived them. He kept his distance from Humphreys which did not diminish the influence of the Outfit, particularly in the election of President Kennedy.

EISENHOWER, Dwight D.
The Commander-in-Chief of American and Allied Forces in Europe in the Second World War, who became Republican President from 1952 to 1960. That he should have met Humphreys and his fellow gangsters in Chicago might seem surprising except that in Chicago politics surprise is an impossible concept.

FISCHETTI, Charles.
A relative of Al Capone's who was very useful to Humphreys in developing gambling in Las Vegas. He later was to be irritating to the Camel by encouraging Sam Giancanna in his relationship with the CIA over Cuba and Castro.

GIANCANNA, Sam.
A busy gunman in his youth and protégé of Humphreys. He became the formal head of the Outfit in the late fifties. He loved the limelight. He became involved in plots to recapture

Cuba or kill Castro. Humphreys is thought to have disapproved of this and certainly he seems to have made no effort to keep Giancanna out of jail. He was probably murdered by colleagues.

GLIMCO, Joseph.
An ally of Humphreys in organising trade unions in Chicago, particularly the Teamsters' Union of which another Humphreys protégé James Hoffa became President. Hoffa was determinedly pursued by Attorney General Kennedy, went to jail and was later murdered.

GUZIK, Jake.
Al Capone's accountant, a man who tried to avoid violence but not always successfully. He became an ally of Humphreys whose wife was to help Guzik with the accounts. Like the Camel, he was a survivor and like all survivors was held to be wise.

KENNA, Michael.
Known as Hinky Dink since he was a small and cheerful man of Irish descent. He became, with his friend the Bath, the controller of the Loop. Although remembered for the style in which he brought corruption in Chicago to a standard hitherto unknown before the First World War, his defenders argue that he made the lives of the new immigrants less miserable than otherwise they would have been. Hinky Dink had style.

THE KENNEDYS.
The father of this important American Catholic family, Joe, was a rival of Humphreys in the bootlegging battles. His son John became President of the United States in 1960, and was murdered in 1963. Another son Robert became Attorney General in his brother's administration. He was murdered in 1968. The Attorney General became a passionate prosecutor of Humphreys and his fellow mobsters. This relationship between the Kennedys and the Outfit is not, unfortunately, beyond belief.

166

LEVEE.
That part of downtown Chicago which towards the end of
the last century and the beginning of this, presented brothels
and gambling dens of a disrepute and elegance the world had
not before seen. What fascinated the visitor was that so much
activity went on within shooting distance of the palaces of
the rich, the new commercial skyscrapers and the hovels of
the new immigrants. When the Levee was cleaned up a little
it became known as the Loop.

LIBONATI, Roland V.
Chicago lawyer who served first in the Illinois Congress and
later in Washington. Humphreys was arrested at the Congressman's first election where all the gang placed their guns
on the piano. He acted as Humphreys' defence counsel from
time to time, met him in Washington and helped argue
the case for the parole of such of the Camel's colleagues
unfortunate enough to be in jail. Mr Libonati speaks well of
Humphreys and assures the author of his – Libonati's –
ignorance of crime in Chicago.

THE LOOP.
The heart of Chicago's commercial and political wealth takes
its name from the elevated rail road which winds between its
buildings. The Loop incorporates, as the Levee did, the First
Ward which was to be the political stronghold of Humphreys
and his precursors, Hinky Dink and Bath House.

McGURK, Jack.
Known as Machine Gun and one of the most reckless killers
employed by Capone. Once tried to kill the entertainer, Joe
E. Lewis, because he had been offered a contract with a night
club in Chicago other than the one controlled by the Outfit.
Capone apologised and paid for the operation to restore the
singer's vocal cords.

MORAN, Bugs.
A friend of O'Banion. Sometimes an ally and sometimes a
rival of Al Capone's. It was Moran's attempt to play a joke
on the Capone mob which is held to have produced the St
Valentine Day Massacre in 1929.

NITTI, Frank.
Known as the Enforcer. He was a necessary murderer for Capone and was Humphreys' principal ally when Capone went to jail. Nitti killed himself rather than go to prison in the Hollywood corruption scandal. This unique suicide might have been due to Nitti's distress that his wife had died young.

O'BANION, Dion.
The leader of the Irish mobs, a former altar boy, abandoned ambitions for the Catholic priesthood and instead became one of the most notorious murderers. When he attempted to seize power the Capone mob killed him and so ensured their triumph. Humphreys, who began his career like O'Banion, selling newspapers, is thought to have found the Irishman's fate instructive.

SIEGEL, Benjamin.
Known as Bugsy, who cooperated with Humphreys in arranging for the legalisation of gambling in Nevada with Meyer Lansky and Sam Giancanna, and who began work setting up casinos in the Caribbean and Middle East. He fell out with the Mafia over a deal in Las Vegas. They murdered him.

STEVENSON, Adlai.
Governor of Illinois and the nominee of the Democratic party for the Presidency in 1952 and 1956. A member of the Chicago Democratic machine although his world-wide repute was of a high-minded, liberal wit. He lost both elections to General Eisenhower and failed to win the Democratic nomination in 1960, partly because Mayor Daley of Chicago decided to abandon him for Senator Kennedy whose subsequent narrow victory Chicago notoriously arranged.

THOMPSON, William.
Known as Big Bill. He won three elections as Mayor of Chicago as a Republican. He was a super American patriot, sportsman and clown. He personified the braggadocio

Chicagoans often fell for. One year he was for the gangs
another year against them, but always won their support
until, in the end, the Democrats pulled themselves together
and defeated Thompson in 1931. His successor, Mayor
Cermak, was assassinated.

TORRIO, John.
Brought in by Big Jim Colosimo to handle his affairs. He
is suspected of murdering his patron. Torrio organised
Chicago to meet the challenge of Prohibition. In turn he
brought in Al Capone from New York, but soon found
that his protégé's dynamism fractured the cool steel of
the Torrio approach. Torrio, like Humphreys later, saw no
reason for indiscriminate violence. Capone's antics and the
warfare that led to Torrio's almost being murdered, persuaded him to return to the more peaceful life of crime in
New York.

TUOHY, Roger.
A minor but successful bootlegger in the twenties, Tuohy
joined the Democrat campaign of Mayor Cermak. He is
believed to have been framed by Humphreys and so spent
twenty-five years in jail. When he was released in 1959 he
was murdered in Chicago after publishing his autobiogra-
phy. Humphreys' alibi is held to have been a classic.

WEINSHANK, Al.
Until the arrival of Humphreys in the laundry business was
one of the most important trade union figures in Chicago.
He joined Bugs Moran's gang and was murdered in the
St Valentine Day Massacre.

Bibliography

Allsop, Kenneth. *The Bootleggers*. London: Hutchinson, 1961

Boyer, Richard O., and Morais, Herbert M. *A History of the American Labour Movement*. London: John Calder, 1955

Dedmon, Emmett. *Fabulous Chicago*. London: Hamish Hamilton, 1953

Demaris, Ovid. *Captive City*.

Giancanna, Antoinette and Renner, Thomas C. *Mafia Princess*. New York: William Morrow, 1984

Hecht, Ben. *A Child of the Century*. New York: Simon & Schuster, 1954

—. *Charlie*. New York: Harper & Brothers, 1957

Jones, Eirwen. *Folk Tales of Wales*. London: Thomas Nelson, 1947

Jones, Gwyn (ed.). *The Oxford Book of Welsh Verse in English*. Oxford University Press, 1977

Kefauver, Estes. *Crime in America*. London: Gollancz, 1952

Kobler, John. *Capone*. London: Michael Joseph, 1972

Lerner, Max. *The Unfinished Country*. London: Weidenfeld & Nicolson, 1959

Machiavelli, Niccolò. (Translated by Peter Bondonella and Mark Musa.) *The Prince*. Oxford University Press, 1984

Morgan, Kenneth O. *Rebirth of a Nation: Wales 1880–1980*. Oxford: Clarendon Press, 1981

Pasley, Fred D. *Al Capone: the Biography of a Self-Made Man*. London: Faber, 1931

Peterson, Virgil W. *Barbarians in our Midst*. Boston: Little, Brown, 1952

Rees, Goronwy. *The Great Slump*. London: Weidenfeld & Nicolson, 1970

Royko, Mike. *Boss, Mayor Richard J. Daley of Chicago.* London: Barrie & Jenkins, 1971

Shannon, William V. *The Heir Apparent: Robert Kennedy and the Struggle for Power.* London: Macmillan, 1967

Terkel, Studs. *Division Street America.* London: Allen Lane the Penguin Press, 1968

Thomas, Bob. *King Cohn.* London: Barrie & Rockliff, 1967

Thomas, Brinley. *Migration and Economic Growth.* Cambridge University Press, 1954

Tuohy, Roger. *The Stolen Years.* New York: Pennington, 1959

Williams, Gwyn A. *The Welsh in their History.* London: Croom Helm, 1982

Wilson, Edmund. *The American Earthquake.* London: W. H. Allen, 1958

Index

175